HarperCollins*Publishers*

YOUR COLLINS TRAVELLER

Your Collins Traveller Guide will help you find your way around your chosen destination quickly and easily. It is colour-coded for easy reference:

The blue section answers the question 'I would like to see or do something; where do I go and what do I see when I get there?' This section is arranged as an alphabetical list of topics. It is recommended that an up-to-date atlas or street plan is used in conjunction with the location maps in this section. Within each topic you will find:

- A selection of the best examples on offer.
- How to get there, costs and opening hours for each entry.
- The outstanding features of each entry.
- A simplified map, with each entry plotted and the nearest landmark or transport access.

The red section is a lively and informative gazetteer. It offers:

- Essential facts about the main places and cultural items. What is La Bastille? Who was Michelangelo? Where is Delphi?

The gold section is full of practical and invaluable travel information. It offers:

- Everything you need to know to help you enjoy yourself and get the most out of your time away, from Accommodation through Baby-sitters, Car Hire, Food, Health, Money, Newspapers, Taxis, Telephones to Youth Hostels.

PRICES	Inexpensive	Moderate	Expensive
Attractions			
Museums, etc.	under 400 Drs	400-800 Drs	over 800 Drs
Restaurants			
Meal, exc. wine	under 1000 Drs	1000-2000 Drs	over 2000 Drs
Nightclubs			
Entry and drink	under 500 Drs	500-1000 Drs	over 1000 Drs

Knossos

Cross-references:

Type in small capitals – **CHURCHES** – tells you that more information on an item is available within the topic on churches.

A-Z after an item tells you that more information is available within the gazetteer. Simply look under the appropriate name.

A name in bold – **Holy Cathedral** – also tells you that more information on an item is available in the gazetteer – again simply look up the name.

CONTENTS

CONTENTS

PRACTICAL INFORMATION GAZETTEER

INTRODUCTION

The island of Crete is a continent in miniature. In the course of one day you can cross a breathtaking mountain range, wander through an orange grove in the throbbing heat of the coastal plain, and slide thankfully into a clear, blue-green sea at a shady beach. It is an island rich in scenic contrasts and redolent with the history of 5000 years.

Crete is the largest and most southerly of the Greek islands, and the fourth-largest in the Mediterranean, lying almost equidistant from mainland Greece and the Turkish and North African coasts. Its long, thin shape provides about 650 miles of coastline, and its long, blazing summers ensure its popularity as a major tourist centre.

When you arrive on Crete, whether by sea or air, the first thing that strikes you is the ruggedness of the treeless terrain. In almost every direction you look there are massive, brooding mountains shimmering in the haze. The spectacular White Mountains (Lefka Ori) lie to the west. Mount Ida (Psiloritis), often snow-capped as late as May, dominates the central range, and the Dikti Mountains, with the famous cave said to be the birthplace of Zeus, king of the Olympian gods, are further east. Lying on a hot beach within reach of the cooling sea, you might feel it too great an effort to struggle up into the mountains but the effort once made is well repaid – the views are awesome and ever-changing, the breezes cool, and the rock and sky fuse in the brilliant light. The mountain roads swoop round bends into tiny olive groves, past villages of whitewashed houses which cling to the mountainside. Although Crete is largely mountainous, the coastal and upland plains are often unexpectedly green and lush, with intensive crops of tomatoes and melons.

The island has many beaches to please sun-loving people, from wide sweeps of dark golden sand to secluded rocky coves. If you have transport, or are prepared to walk, it is still possible, particularly on the south coast, to find undeveloped beaches with few visitors.

Crete has had a long and turbulent history and, it must be remembered, has only been part of Greece since 1913. Before then the island was in the hands of the Turks for two and a half centuries, and before that there were four centuries of Venetian rule. In fact, ever since the decline of the great Minoan civilization, possession of Crete has been

fiercely contested. The island was taken by Rome in 67 BC, by Byzantium in AD 395, by the Arabs in 824, retaken by Byzantium in 961, and sold to the Venetians in 1204 for 1000 silver marks. But Cretans have always resisted invaders forcefully. Throughout the centuries they have risen in rebellion against their various overlords, as was also demonstrated in World War II during the German invasion of the island, when many Cretans took to the mountains and, along with their allies, waged guerilla warfare to regain their freedom. Out of this rich and diverse past the Minoan civilization stands supreme. Flourishing

c. 2500-1400 BC, the Minoans created a distinctive culture that is regarded as Europe's first great civilization. Their palaces and frescoes, their pottery and jewellery were unrivalled in the ancient world, and the kingdom of Minos, with its extensive trade links, held sway over most of the Aegean. But the dividing line between history and legend is often hazy. Was Minos one king or the name of many kings? What exactly was the dreaded Minotaur, said to be half man, half beast (the result of an unnatural lust for a bull wished on Minos' wife by a vindictive god)? One of the frescoes in Herakļion's Archaeological Museum shows a slim bull-leaper vaulting gracefully over the horns of a bull. Was this a sport, or a ritual performed by the young sacrificial victims before being devoured by the Minotaur?
There is so much to see on Crete: archaeological sites from Minoan and later periods, Byzantine monasteries and churches with their beautiful icons, Venetian fortresses, huge and impressive caves, spectacular

mountain gorges – it would take a year to see and appreciate everything. But above all, the visitor should try to visit the two great Minoan palaces at Knossos and Phaestos. Go first to the world-renowned Archaeological Museum in Heraklion and view the wonderful Minoan artefacts from the sites before going to Knossos itself, just 5 km away, to see the partly reconstructed palace. Visiting the palace of Phaestos, in the south of the island, will take up a whole day, leaving from Heraklion, but the beauty of its setting is unsurpassed.

Crete undoubtedly has something for everyone. With the increase in tourist developments many of the towns and resorts have acquired quite a cosmopolitan air, with Continental-style restaurants, souvenir and craft shops, and fashionable bars and discos. But still the contrasts persist. Behind the hurly-burly of Rethymnon and Chania's lively seafronts there are the charming, narrow streets of the old Venetian quarters, where minarets and shells of Venetian *palazzi* bear witness to Crete's turbulent past.

If your preference is for a sun and sea holiday, there are many busy resorts offering all kinds of entertainment, from water sports and boat trips to inland coach tours. For the energetic there is the 18 km trek through the spectacular gorge of Samaria and walks in the mountains or along the dramatic southwest coast, where the mountains seem to plunge straight into the sea. But take care and go well prepared – Crete is a rugged place.

Tourism has inevitably left its mark on this most Greek of Greek islands and its proud and hospitable people. The north coast, in particular, is heavily developed in many places, and some formerly quiet fishing villages in the south now throng with summer visitors. But ancient traditions die hard and Crete is a big island. Off the beaten track in the less frequented coastal and mountain villages, the visitor's few words of Greek – *kalimera* (good morning), *efkaristo* (thank you) – will be greeted with welcoming smiles and hospitality. If you can, it is worth hiring a car for a few days to cross one of the mountain ranges, perhaps taking in a monastery or Minoan site along the way, and heading for one of the more remote villages on the south coast, where you can sit in a taverna by the beach with a glass or two of retsina or a cool beer, a plate of grilled red mullet and a Greek salad, and watch the sun sinking lazily into the Aegean Sea.

Days on Crete pass very pleasantly, and however you spend your time – swimming, sunning or exploring – you will not easily forget what Homer called this 'land of Crete in the midst of the wine-dark sea'.

Gulf of Mirabello
SPINALONGA
Elounda
Neapolis
Heraklion
Archanes
Kastelli
Malia
AGIOS NIKOLAOS CHAPEL
VOULISMENI LAKE
Agios Nikolaos
LATO
KRITSA
MONI FANEROMENI
Males
Ierapetra
GOURNIA
Ano Viannos
Agii Deka
Sitia
Vai
ZAKROS

VOULISMENI LAKE Off the harbour in Agios Nikolaos.
The so-called 'bottomless' lake is actually only some 60 m deep and is just a rather murky inner harbour. It looks prettier at night.

AGIOS NIKOLAOS CHAPEL On the road to Elounda.
Check with tourist office for opening times.
An 8th or 9thC chapel dedicated to the patron saint of mariners (St. Nicholas), from which the town derived its name, with interesting frescoes.

SPINALONGA Off Elounda.
Regular boat trips from Agios Nikolaos and Elounda.
Island fortress which served as leper colony earlier this century. See **A-Z**.

KRITSA 11 km southwest of Agios Nikolaos.
Bus hourly 0630-1930.
Large picturesque village well known as a handicrafts centre. See **A-Z**.

LATO 3 km from Kritsa along a well-signposted track.
0800-1500 Tue.-Sun. Inexpensive.
Doric remains from the 5th-3rdC BC. Magnificent views of the sea and mountains.

ZAKROS 45 km southeast of Sitia.
0830-1500. Bus from Sitia 1100. Expensive.
The ruins of a Minoan palace. See **AGIOS NIKOLAOS-EXCURSION 1**, **A-Z**.

GOURNIA 19 km southeast of Agios Nikolaos.
0830-1500 Tue.-Sun. Hourly bus from Agios Nikolaos. Free.
Well-preserved remains of a Minoan town. You can see most of it clearly from the road. See **A-Z**.

MONI FANEROMENI East of Agios Nikolaos near Gournia.
0800-1400. Hourly bus then a steep climb.
Byzantine convent built around a 'miraculous' grotto. There are fine views towards the gulf.

Gulf of Mirabello
Heraklion
Archanes
Kastelli
Malia
Neapolis
ELOUNDA
AGIOS NIKOLAOS
AMOUDHARA
ISTRO
Males
Ano Viannos
Agii Deka
MIRTOS
IERAPETRA
FERMA
SITIA
VAI
Zakros

AGIOS NIKOLAOS

AGIOS NIKOLAOS Bus, foot.
Four busy beaches near the town. Both Ammos and the municipal beach are small and shingly. There are sandy beaches at Ammoudi 10 min to the north and Almiros 2 km south.

ELOUNDA 11 km north of Agios Nikolaos. Regular bus.
Shallow, pebbly bays with clear water which is ideal for snorkelling. Submerged city.

AMOUDHARA 5 km south of Agios Nikolaos.
KTEL Sitia/Ierapetra bus.
Clear, quiet, sandy beach easily reached from the road. Tavernas nearby.

ISTRO 9 km south of Agios Nikolaos near Kalo Horio. KTEL bus.
Small, pleasant, sandy beaches a few minutes from the road.

SITIA 70 km east of Agios Nikolaos. KTEL Sitia bus.
Long, busy, sandy beach. A bit dirty but with cafés nearby. *See* AGIOS NIKOLAOS-EXCURSION 1.

VAI 23 km northeast of Sitia. Daily bus from Sitia.
Short and very crowded sandy stretch with palm trees. *See* AGIOS NIKOLAOS-EXCURSION 1.

IERAPETRA 36 km south of Agios Nikolaos. Regular bus.
Long gritty beach by this sizable south coast resort. *See* AGIOS NIKOLAOS-EXCURSION 1, A-Z.

FERMA 10 km east of Ierapetra.
One of several coves here with clean, clear water.

MIRTOS 15 km west of Ierapetra. Bus from Ierapetra.
Long, clean beach of dark sand and shingle beside attractive village.

Gulf of Mirabello
Heraklion
Archanes
Agii Deka
Kastelli
Malia
Ano Viannos
Males
Neapolis
Elounda
AGIOS NIKOLAOS
IERAPETRA
VASILIKI
KAVOUSI
MOHLOS
SFAKA
KHAMEZI
SITIA
EPANO EPISKOPI
ANALIPSI
EITA
NEA PRISOS
PALEKASTRO
MONI TOPLOU
VAI
ZAKROS

Excursion 1

This excursion can be done either as one long one (241 km), or two slightly shorter ones of 205 km and 232 km, taking in Sitia, Moni Toplou, Vai and Palekastro (and possibly Zakros), Nea Prisos, Etia, Analipsi, Ierapetra and Vasiliki. Directions and distances are given for the longest excursion.

Take the main road out of Agios Nikolaos towards Sitia.
26 km – Kavousi. A pretty, tree-lined village with spectacular views of the coast and the mountains to the west.
40 km – Sfaka. Take a detour from here down the road to the left, sign-posted Mohlos.
48 km – Mohlos. A tiny fishing village with tavernas, and rooms to rent. There are Minoan ruins here and on the islands of Psira and Mohlos (see **A-Z**) across the bay. Return to Sfaka and rejoin the main road, heading east towards Sitia.
65 km – Khamezi. Just before the village there are the remains of an oval Minoan building, the original function of which is in doubt. Khamezi was also the probable birthplace of the 17thC writer Vincent Kornaros, author of the great epic poem, *Erotokritos*. There is a small museum of antiquities just outside the village.
75 km – Sitia (see **AGIOS NIKOLAOS-BEACHES**). A modern harbour town with a relaxed atmosphere. There are lots of tavernas along the seafront (Zorba's is one of the better ones and has clean toilets), and there are also two small museums in the town and the remains of a Venetian fort. Continue on the road east out of Sitia and turn off to the left after 14 km, signposted Moni Toplou.
90 km – Moni Toplou (see **A-Z**). Continue travelling east along the same road to Vai.
99 km – Vai (see **AGIOS NIKOLAOS-BEACHES**). The small beach here is famous for its grove of palm trees but it does get very crowded with coach parties. There are café-bars and fruit stalls, and umbrellas and beach beds for hire. Return to the junction and turn left for Palekastro.
111 km – Palekastro. Take the unsurfaced road to the beach here and you will find sheltered sand, three small, family-run tavernas and very few people – a good place to relax, swim and have some lunch. Behind the shore are the ruins of one of the largest Minoan cities ever found

Moni Toplou

Sitia

but they are not easy to make out.

DETOUR: Zakros (see **AGIOS NIKOLAOS-ATTRACTIONS, A-Z**) is some 25 km south of Palekastro and can be visited as an extension of this excursion. Return to Sitia (130 km).

For the first shorter excursion, return to Agios Nikolaos from here (205 km). For the second shorter excursion return to Sitia from Palekastro and continue with the directions for the long excursion. Turn south when you get back to Sitia, following the signs for Ierapetra. Drive through the villages of Piskokefalo and Maronia.

144 km – Epano Episkopi. A pleasant little town below the White Mountains. Turn left just beyond the village, signposted Ziros.

149 km – Nea Prisos. There are some remains here of a city said to be the last stronghold of the Minoan culture. Rejoin the main road south and after 6 km fork left.

160 km – Etia. Some fine Venetian aristocratic residences have survived here. Return to the main road.

172 km – Analipsi. The first little harbour town you reach on the coast, Analipsi has suffered only low-key development and has several quiet tavernas on the seafront.

204 km – Ierapetra (see **AGIOS NIKOLAOS-BEACHES, A-Z**). Follow signs for Agios Nikolaos, taking the northern road out of the town.

215 km – Vasiliki. The site of a small pre-Minoan settlement dating from c. 2500 BC. The village has given its name to Vasiliki ware, a distinctive semi-lustrous pottery found here. Continue north to the coastal road and turn left to return to Agios Nikolaos (241 km).

Limin Chersonisos
Spinalonga
MALIA
Neapolis
POTAMIES
Aposelemis
KRASI
TZERMIADO
KERA
Gonies
AVDOU
Kastelli
Lagou
AGIOS NIKOLAOS
Gulf of Mirabello
LASITHI PLATEAU
Mesa Lasithi
AGIOS GEORGIOS
Psychro
DIKTAEAN CAVE

Excursion 2

A one-day excursion to the Lasithi Plateau (see **A-Z***) in the Dikti Mountains, taking in the villages of Potamies, Avdou, Krasi, Tzermiado and Psychro, and visiting the famous Diktaean Cave. The path inside the cave is very slippery so you must have suitable footwear, warm clothing and a torch, though candles are on sale.*

From Agios Nikolaos take the main road northwest towards Heraklion, through the bustling resort of Malia (see **HERAKLION-BEACHES**) after 32 km, then turn left (inland) after a further 12 km, just beyond Limin Chersonisos. Follow the road for 6 km before taking the left-hand fork through the green valley of the river Aposelemis.

55 km – Potamies. Just before the village turn left (signposted) to the deserted monastery of Panagia Gouverniotissa, still decorated with 14thC frescoes. The Byzantine church of Christos, in the village itself, has more frescoes from the 14th-15thC (you will have to ask in the village for the keys). Continue towards the mountains.

60 km – Avdou. There are more churches of interest in and around this unspoilt village, including Agios Antonios, Agios Georgios and Agios Konstantinos (1 km southwest), all of which have beautiful 14thC frescoes. There is a lovely shady taverna, the Minore, on the left just beyond Avdou – it's an excellent place for an iced coffee and has good toilets. Some 4 km beyond the village of Gonies there is a fork in the road: keep right to continue the climb; turn left and you will find yourself in the narrow streets of Krasi.

67 km – Krasi. An attractive village with shady plane trees; the best tavernas are at the top of the town.

70 km – Kera. Just before the village turn left to the monastery of Panagia Kera (also known as Kardiotissa), which has some well-preserved Byzantine frescoes which have only recently been uncovered (0800-1400). The views are spectacular from here – on a clear day you can see Heraklion. Carry on up to the rim of the plateau and stop in the car park. Climb up to the row of ruined stone windmills, which used to grind cereals, for a superb view of the plateau with its still-working windmills, pumping water for the irrigation of the patchwork of fields. Drive down onto the plateau and turn left.

79 km – Tzermiado. The villagers here try to catch the passing tourist trade with their woven rugs, crochet work and embroidery, much of it displayed in the street. Continue to Psychro.

91 km – Psychro. Follow the signs for the Diktaean Cave (see **A-Z**). It is a 20 min walk from the car park to the cave entrance (0800-1800; Moderate; guides 2000 Drs; donkey to entrance 1500 Drs). Return to Psychro and turn right towards Agios Georgios.

96 km – Agios Georgios. There is a small folklore museum here. At Agios Constandinos fork right to Mesa Lasithi and follow the signs for Agios Nikolaos (133 km).

View from Kera

Lasithi Plateau

Akti S. Koundourou
DILINI
Koritsas
K. Paleologou
Koraka
AQUARIUS
Harbour
LOOK-
IN
Lake
Voulismeni
SKY
LINE
Akti I. Koundourou
BARA
BARA
KAHLUA
Pasifais
N. Plastira
DIONYSSOS
Filelinon
28 Octovriou
Roussou Koundourou
25 Martiou
SCORPIO
M. Sfakianaki
Akti Pagaloun
Kitroplatia
Iroon Politekniou
K. Sfakianaki
Platia
Venizelou
Kontogiani
S. Venizelou
Platia
Atlandithos
Kosirii

Nightlife

See **Opening Times**.

BARA BARA Akti I. Koundourou.
On the eastern side of the harbour. ● Expensive.
Very popular disco, with videos and good lighting.

SKY LINE Akti I. Koundourou.
On the quayside towards the ferry terminal. ● Expensive.
Fashionable disco with a good selection of music.

SCORPIO 25 Martiou Street.
Just up from the harbour. ● Moderate.
A popular disco which gets extremely crowded in the summer.

KAHLUA 25 Martiou Street.
Near the Scorpio disco (see above). ● Moderate.
Trendy bar with a young clientele. Good music.

LOOK-IN N. Plastira Street.
Above Lake Voulismeni. ● Moderate.
Atmospheric bar with good pop music.

AQUARIUS Akti S. Koundourou.
On the harbourfront towards Ammoudi. ● Moderate.
Pseudo-British pub with lively atmosphere and exotic cocktails.

DILINI Ammoudi.
On the left at the end of the promenade. ● Moderate.
Excellent atmosphere and good food, as well as different types of music, including bouzouki and Greek dancing.

DIONYSSOS Limnes.
10 km northwest on the Heraklion road. ● Moderate.
Bouzouki and Cretan music. Good atmosphere. Tours available.

ORMOS
KRISTALLO
AMMOUDI
Akti S. Koundourou
IKAROS
Koritsas
K. Paleologou
Koraka
ZEPHIROS
Harbour
Lake
Voulismeni
Akti I. Koundourou
ARIADNE
N. Plastira
Platia
Venizelou
Filelinon
28th Octovriou
Roussou Koundourou
25 Martiou
M. Sfakianaki
Pasifais
DELTA
Akti Pagaloun
TRATA
Kitroplatia
K. Sfakianaki
Iroon Politekniou
ITANOS
S. Ven zelou
Kontogiani
Platia
Atlandithos
Kosirii

ORMOS Ammoudi.
On the road to the promontory. ■ Lunch and evening. ● Expensive.
Quality hotel restaurant with Greek and international menu, and occasional bouzouki music.

ARIADNE Akti I. Koundourou.
Beside the harbour. ■ Lunch and evening. ● Expensive.
Family-run establishment offering quality dishes. Popular with tourists.

KRISTALLO Ammoudi.
Just past the Mirabello Hotel. ■ All day. ● Moderate.
Traditional taverna with good Greek music and occasional dancing.

ZEPHIROS Akti S. Koundourou.
On the harbourfront. ■ All day. ● Moderate.
Popular with tourists from breakfast through until late.

ITANOS Kyprou Street 1.
Just off the central square. ■ All day. ● Moderate.
There's a family atmosphere in this traditional restaurant.

TRATA Mihali Sfakianaki Street 14.
Just back from the seafront. ■ All day. ● Moderate.
Pretty roof garden with candle-lit tables in the evening. Good food.

AMMOUDI Ammoudi.
10 min from the town centre at the beach. ■ All day. ● Moderate.
Waterfront taverna serving the usual dishes and good fish.

DELTA Kitroplatia.
Behind the beach. ■ All day. ● Moderate.
Friendly modern taverna with international and Greek menus.

IKAROS Akti S. Koundourou 25.
Behind the promenade. ■ All day. ● Moderate.
Family-run with a great atmosphere. Where the locals come to eat.

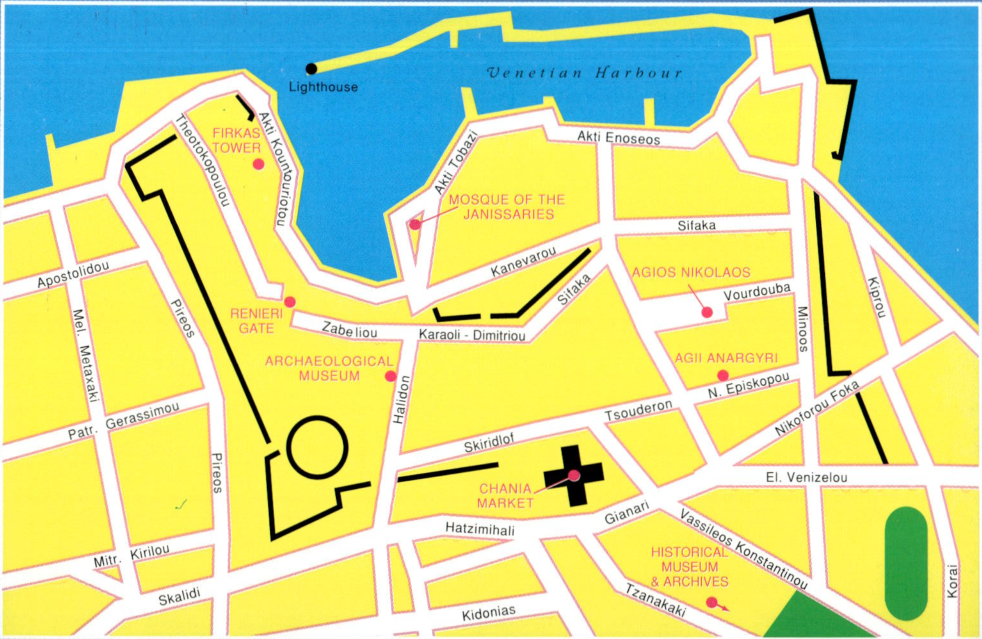

Venetian Harbour
Lighthouse
FIRKAS TOWER
Akti Kountouriotou
Theotokopoulou
MOSQUE OF THE JANISSARIES
Akti Tobazi
Akti Enoseos
Sifaka
Kanevarou
Sifaka
AGIOS NIKOLAOS
Vourdouba
Minoos
Kiprou
RENIERI GATE
Zabeliou
Karaoli - Dimitriou
ARCHAEOLOGICAL MUSEUM
Halidon
AGII ANARGYRI
N. Episkopou
Nikoforou Foka
Tsouderon
Skiridlof
CHANIA MARKET
El. Venizelou
Gianari
Vassileos Konstantinou
HISTORICAL MUSEUM & ARCHIVES
Tzanakaki
Korai
Hatzimihali
Kidonias
Skalidi
Mitr. Kirilou
Patr. Gerassimou
Mel. Metaxaki
Apostolidou
Pireos
Pireos
Pireos

OLD CITY, VENETIAN HARBOUR & LIGHTHOUSE
The chief interest and charm of Chania lies in the Venetian harbour with its lighthouse, and in the old quarter with its picturesque squares and fountains, handsome buildings and waterfront cafés.

FIRKAS TOWER At the entrance to the outer harbour.
The tower houses the Naval Museum of Crete (1000-1800 Tue.-Sun.; Inexpensive). Theatre and displays are held in the courtyard during the summer, e.g. folk dancing every Tue., Thu. & Sun. at 2100 (Expensive).

RENIERI GATE Moshon Street.
Elegant archway embellished with a coat of arms and 17thC inscription.

MOSQUE OF THE JANISSARIES On the harbourfront.
17thC mosque in the throes of restoration. The NTOG (see **Tourist Information***) has moved until these are completed.*

AGIOS NIKOLAOS CHURCH Splanzia quarter.
Converted by the Turks in the 17thC when it was renamed after Sultan Ibrahim. A fine minaret stands beside the Greek Orthodox campanile.

AGII ANARGYRI CHURCH Splanzia quarter.
Orthodox church containing splendid Byzantine frescoes and icons.

CHANIA MARKET Hatzimihali Street/Tsouderon Street.
Built in the shape of a cross, this bustling covered market has stalls selling all kinds of regional food and crafts. See **Chania**.

ARCHAEOLOGICAL MUSEUM Halidon Street.
0800-1900 Tue.-Sun. (closes earlier in winter). Moderate.
Housed in the restored Venetian church of Agios Francisko. Minoan pottery, sarcophagi, inscribed tablets, classical sculpture, mosaics. See **A-Z**.

HISTORICAL MUSEUM & ARCHIVES Sfakianaki Street 20.
Near the public gardens. 0900-1800 Tue.-Sun. Moderate.
Relics relating to the Cretan struggle for independence against Turkey.

STAVROS
Akrotiri
KALATHAS
FALASARNA
Kastelli
PLATANIAS
Platanos
AGIA
MARINA
KALAMAKI
Chania
CHANIA CITY
(NEA CHORA)
KALIVES
Perama
Rethymnon
PALEOCHORA
Chora Sfakion
FRANGOKASTELLO
Selia
Spili
Agia Galini

FALASARNA 59 km west of Chania.
Car or bus to Platanos, then 5 km walk.
Superb sweep of golden sand in a sheltered bay.

PLATANIAS 10 km west of Chania.
Popular stretch of grey sand and shingle. Exposed in places.

AGIA MARINA 8 km west of Chania.
Local bus.
A busy, sandy beach with outcrops of rock. Water-sport facilities.

KALAMAKI 5 km west of Chania.
Blue city bus.
Sheltered, sandy beach with shallow water popular for swimming.

CHANIA CITY BEACH (NEA CHORA)
10 min walk west of the harbour.
A long, crowded, sandy beach with plenty of amenities. Less crowded further along.

KALATHAS & STAVROS 12 km and 16 km northeast of Chania.
Bus from Chania.
Two sandy beaches on the Akrotiri peninsula.

KALIVES 20 km east of Chania.
Long, sandy beach on either side of sprawling village with tavernas and places to stay.

FRANGOKASTELLO 12 km east of Chora Sfakion.
Daily bus from Chania in summer.
Lovely beach beneath the castle ruins. Clear, shallow water. *See* **A-Z**.

PALEOCHORA 80 km southwest of Chania.
Daily bus (journey takes 2 hr).
Magnificent tree-lined sand and steeply-shelving shingle beaches with cafés and tavernas on either side of the resort. *See* **CHANIA-EXCURSION**.

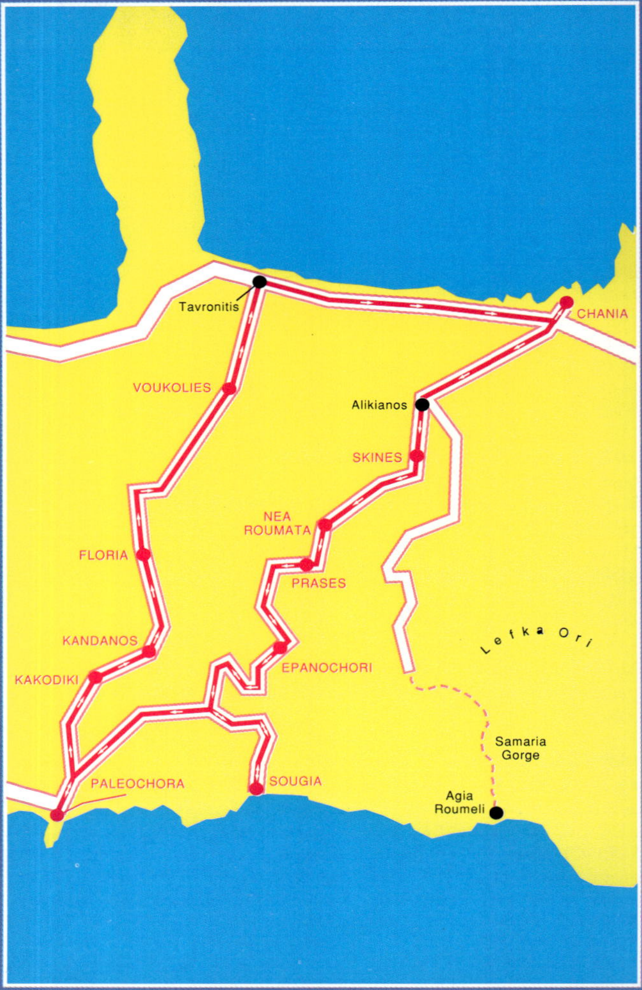

Tavronitis
CHANIA
VOUKOLIES
Alikianos
SKINES
NEA
ROUMATA
FLORIA
PRASES
Lefka Ori
KANDANOS
EPANOCHORI
KAKODIKI
Samaria
Gorge
PALEOCHORA
SOUGIA
Agia
Roumeli

Excursion

A one-day excursion to the delightful south coast town of Paleochora through the mountain villages of Skines, Prases and Agia Irini, and back through Kakodiki, Kandanos, Floria and Voukolies. If you want to see the Sat. morning market at Voukolies, you should do the excursion in reverse.

Leave Chania southwest towards Alikianos, keeping left after 16 km when you reach the village, following signs for Sougia.
20 km – Skines. As you start to climb the foothills of the Lefka Or range, Skines is a pretty village lined with tavernas and shady trees. The countryside is wonderfully green, almost lush, with running streams all year round, birdsong and orange groves.
33 km – Nea Roumata. The scenery now becomes almost alpine, with steep limestone gorges and pine trees.
35 km – Prases. There are a couple of welcoming tavernas here, the start of chestnut-growing country.
47 km – Agia Irini. Another spectacular gorge off to the left gives you a glimpse of the kind of scenery to be expected around the Samaria Gorge (see **A-Z**) nearby.
50 km – Epanochori. A taverna and lonely chapel mark your first sighting of the Libyan Sea. There is often a tremendous wind funnelling through here, so hold on to your hat! Keep following Sougia signs.
DETOUR: After 11 km turn left for another 11 km to Sougia. The drive down is tortuous but this small resort is sufficiently remote to have remained quiet and relatively unspoilt.
If you don't feel like making the detour, keep right at the junction towards Paleochora.
69 km – Temenia. The signposting is confusing here. Keep left (don't go through Temenia itself) and take the more direct route to Paleochora.
95 km – Paleochora (see **CHANIA-BEACHES**). If you can face more mountain driving, there is a spectacular road round the western mountains through Voutas and Topolia, but it is suggested that you return by the better road.
107 km – Kakodiki. Tradition has it that there are curative springs here.
114 km – Kandanos. Stop by the war memorial below the church, which reads, 'Here stood Kandanos, destroyed in revenge for the

deaths of 25 German soldiers'. It has mostly been rebuilt but is still a stark reminder of the horrors of World War II.

124 km – Floria. Another two war memorials and two Byzantine churches, both with frescoes. The tavernas are all suitably flower-bedecked. After 4 km a spectacular gorge opens up on your left before you start to drop down to the north coast.

145 km – Voukolies. There is a huge and crowded Sat. morning market here selling everything from chickens to plastic buckets.

151 km – Tavronitis. Turn right at the T-junction with the main east–west trunk road. It is then 25 km back to Chania (176 km).

Chania

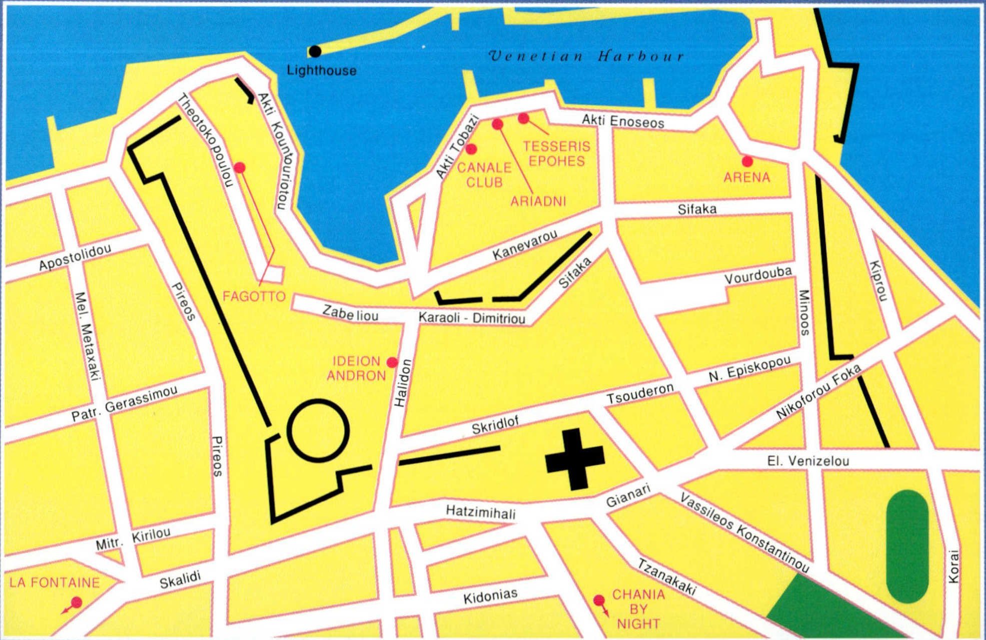

Venetian Harbour
Lighthouse
Akti Kountouriotou
Theotokopoulou
Akti Tobazi
Akti Enoseos
CANALE CLUB
TESSERIS EPOHES
ARIADNI
ARENA
Sifaka
Kanevarou
Sifaka
Vourdouba
Minoos
Kiprou
Apostolidou
FAGOTTO
Zabeliou
Karaoli - Dimitriou
Mel. Metaxaki
Pireos
IDEION ANDRON
Halidon
N. Episkopou
Tsouderon
Nikoforou Foka
Patr. Gerassimou
Skridlof
Pireos
El. Venizelou
Gianari
Hatzimihali
Vassileos Konstantinou
Mitr. Kirilou
LA FONTAINE
Skalidi
Kidonias
Tzanakaki
CHANIA BY NIGHT
Korai

See **Opening Times**.

IDEION ANDRON Halidon Street.
Next to the Archaeological Museum. ● Expensive.
Friendly open-air cocktail bar. Good, sometimes live, music.

ARIADNI Akti Tobazi 19.
By the old port. ● Expensive.
Very popular air-conditioned disco with modern décor.

TESSERIS EPOHES (FOUR SEASONS) Akti Tobazi 26.
By the old port. ● Expensive.
Trendy waterside bar serving delicious cocktails to a background of jazz music.

CHANIA BY NIGHT 8 km east of Chania.
North side of New Heraklion Road. Taxi, car. ● Expensive.
The best place to go for bouzouki, cabaret and folk dancing (see **A-Z***).*

FAGOTTO Agelou Street 16.
Behind the Naval Museum to the west of the old port. ● Moderate.
Small and friendly jazz bar with occasional live performances.

ARENA Kalergon Street 11.
South of the outer harbour. ● Moderate.
Small modern bar with music to suit all tastes.

CANALE CLUB Akti Tobazi.
By the old port. ● Moderate.
Another very popular waterside disco with visiting live bands.

LA FONTAINE 17 km west of Chania.
Past the Symposo restaurant on the coast road just west of Maleme.
● Moderate.
Modern disco with cocktail bar and good snacks.

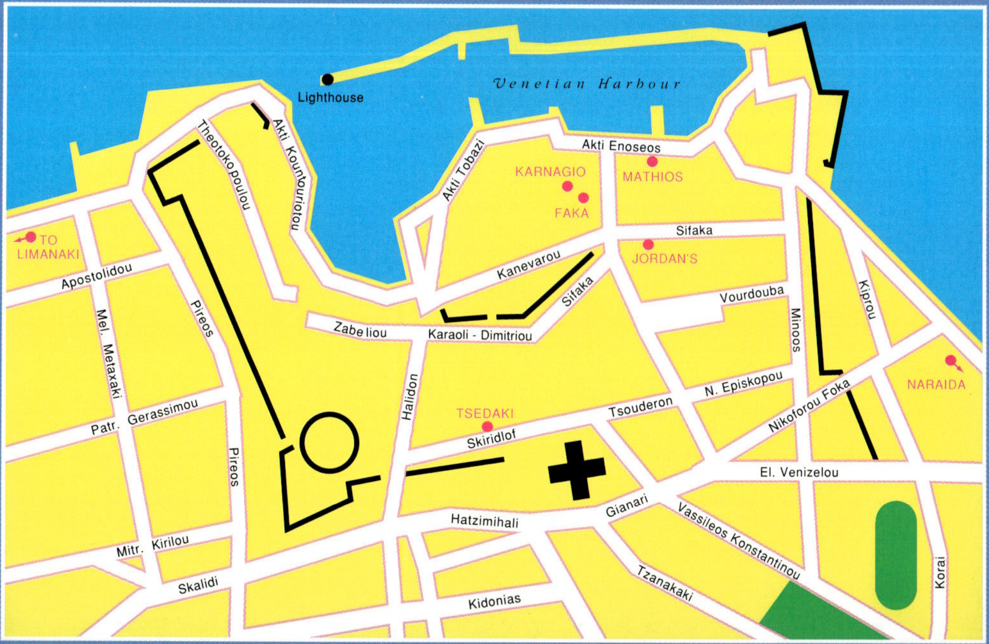
Venetian Harbour
Lighthouse
Akti Kountouriotou
Theotokopoulou
Akti Tobazi
Akti Enoseos
KARNAGIO
FAKA
MATHIOS
Sifaka
JORDAN'S
Kanevarou
Sifaka
Vourdouba
Minoos
Kiprou
NARAIDA
TO LIMANAKI
Apostolidou
Mel. Metaxaki
Pireos
Zabeliou
Karaoli - Dimitriou
Halidon
TSEDAKI
Skiridlof
Tsouderon
N. Episkopou
Nikoforou Foka
El. Venizelou
Patr. Gerassimou
Pireos
Hatzimihali
Gianari
Vassileos Konstantinou
Mitr. Kirilou
Skalidi
Kidonias
Tzanakaki
Korai

Restaurants

NARAIDA Akrotiriou Avenue 119.
4 km from Chania on the Akrotiri road. Taxi. ■ Evenings. ● Expensive.
Elegant restaurant with a veranda overlooking the old town and harbour. Serves traditional Italian and Greek dishes, and good wine.

KARNAGIO Katehaki Square 8.
Back from the old port. ■ Lunch and evening. ● Moderate.
One of the best-value eating places in the area. Tables on the square, a friendly atmosphere and good food.

TO LIMANAKI Akti Kanari 5, Nea Chora.
By the new harbour. ■ Lunch and evening. ● Moderate.
Family-run taverna with friendly service and good dishes of the day – try the lamb with garlic cooked in a paper bag!

MATHIOS Akti Enoseos 3.
By the old port. ■ Lunch and evening. ● Moderate.
Pleasant, quiet, traditional taverna on the waterfront.

FAKA Archoleon Street 15.
Back from the port behind the harbour police office. ■ Lunch and evening (summer). ● Moderate.
Informal restaurant with good service, tables on the square and delicious food.

TSEDAKI Tsouderon 33.
Opposite the entrance to the market. ■ All day. ● Moderate.
Up-market café serving mouthwatering pastries and fresh coffee.

JORDAN'S Sifaka 4.
Blue chairs on the raised sidewalk. ■ All day. ● Inexpensive.
Traditional cheese pie (bougatsa) *topped with sugar and served with a glass of cold water or with coffee from the lady next door. Unbeatable value and absolutely delicious.*

KOULES FORTRESS
Venetian Harbour
Makariou
Sophocles Venizelou
HISTORICAL & ETHNOGRAPHICAL MUSEUM
Epimenidou
25 Avgoustou
AGIOS TITOS
MOROSINI FOUNTAIN
ARCHAEOLOGICAL MUSEUM
Giamalaki
Platia Venizelou
AGIA EKATERINI
AGIOS MARKOS
Bofor
Idis
Makariou
Kalokerinou
Ikarou
AGIOS MINAS
Loukareos
1821
Evans
Platia Eleftherias
Averof
62 Martiron
Porta Chania
Evans
Trikoupi
Nikolaou
Plastira
TOMB OF NIKOS KAZANTZAKIS
Dimokratias
Knosou

Attractions

ARCHAEOLOGICAL MUSEUM Xanthoudidou Street.
■ 0800-1900 Tue.-Sun., 1230-1900 Mon. ● Expensive.
One of Greece's finest museums. Finds from Knossos, Phaestos. See **A-Z**.

HISTORICAL & ETHNOGRAPHICAL MUSEUM Kalokerinou Street. Opposite the Xenia Hotel. ■ 0900-1700 Mon.-Fri., 0900-1400 Sat. ● Moderate.
Interesting collection of frescoes, sculptures, coins. Visit the reconstructed study of Crete's famous author, Nikos Kazantzakis (see **A-Z**). *See* **A-Z**.

TOMB OF NIKOS KAZANTZAKIS Martinengo Bastion.
Imposing tomb of the author of Zorba, *inscribed with the words, 'I hope for nothing. I fear nothing. I am free.'*

KOULES FORTRESS Venetian harbour.
■ 0730-1730 (depending on exhibitions). ● Moderate.
Imposing 16thC Venetian fortress decorated with the Lions of St. Mark.

AGIA EKATERINI Agia Ekaterini Square. ■ 0930-1300 Tue.-Sun., 1700-1900 Tue., Thu., Fri. & Sun. ● Inexpensive.
16thC church housing the excellent Museum of Religious Art. See **A-Z**.

AGIOS MINAS Agia Ekaterini Square. ■ 0730-1800.
This huge 19thC cathedral dominates the tiny original church beside it.

AGIOS TITOS 25 Avgoustou Street. ■ 0700-1200, 1700-2000.
Rebuilt several times, the church has served the Greek Orthodox, Catholic and Islamic faiths. Contains the skull of St. Titus (see **A-Z**).

AGIOS MARKOS Venizelou Square.
Twice damaged by earthquakes, the church was rebuilt by the Venetians and converted into a mosque under the Turks. It now houses reproductions of frescoes.

MOROSINI FOUNTAIN Venizelou (Fountain) Square.
Fine Venetian fountain with marble lions and mythological figures.

Platanos
Chania
Chora Sfakion
Rethymnon
Spili
AGIA PELAGIA
AMOUDHARA
Agia Galini
KOKKINOS PIRGOS
MATALA
TOBROUK
Heraklion
Kastelli
CHERSONISOS
MALIA
Males
Agios
Nikolaos
Ierapetra
Sitia
Zakros

Beaches

CHERSONISOS 29 km east of Heraklion.
Bus from the port.
A small, sandy and fairly clean beach beside this ancient settlement which is now a busy tourist resort. There is nudist bathing in the vicinity (see **Nudism***). See* **A-Z**.

MALIA 32 km east of Heraklion.
Bus from the port.
Popular beach with fine sand and clear, shallow water. Plenty of shops, tavernas and discos in the busy resort. See **AGIOS NIKOLAOS-EXCURSION 2**.

TOBROUK 7 km east of Heraklion near the airport.
Bus 1 from the city centre.
One of the closest beaches to the capital, making it an extremely popular spot. Tavernas and cold drink stands. Quieter areas are further along.

AMOUDHARA 6 km west of Heraklion.
Bus from Porta Chania.
Sandy resort beach which is a bit dirty. You can find more secluded and cleaner spots by walking further west around the bay.

AGIA PELAGIA 15 km west of Heraklion.
Bus from Porta Chania.
Good beaches of sand, rock and pebble on either side of this up-market resort. There are water-sport facilities and sheltered waters.

MATALA 75 km southwest of Heraklion.
Bus from Porta Chania.
Idyllic beach which shelves steeply into the sea at this former hippy haven (now a mainstream tourist development). There are underwater remains and lots of caves.

KOKKINOS PIRGOS 73 km southwest of Heraklion.
Regular bus from Porta Chania.
Beach stretching west towards Agia Galini (see **HERAKLION-EXCURSION 1***), though not the region's most attractive. Popular with local inhabitants.*

Dia
Island
Gulf
of
Heraklion
Perama
HERAKLION
Anogia
NIDA PLAIN
Idaian Cave
PSILORITIS
MONI
VRONDISI
KAMARES
AGIA VARVARA
ZAROS
AGIA
GALINI
Vourvoulitis
AGII DEKA
Gulf
of
Mesara
MESARA PLAIN
PHAESTOS
AGIA
TRIADA

Excursion 1

A one-day excursion to the south, taking in the archaeological and historic sites of Agii Deka, Gortys, Phaestos, Agia Triada, Kamares, Moni Vrondisi and Zaros.

Leave Heraklion in a westerly direction through the Porta Chania (Chania Gate). After 2 km turn left onto the Agia Galini road, heading south towards the lower eastern slopes of Psiloritis (Mount Ida), which is signposted Mires off the bypass.

30 km – Agia Varvara. Situated at a height of 600 m, this is the main village of the region and generally considered to be the geographic centre of the island. Continue south along the main road as it climbs to its highest point, bypassing Vourvoulitis, before descending in a series of hairpin bends to the Mesara plain.

45 km – Agii Deka ('Holy Ten'). This is the first village you come to on the fertile plain. Ten Christians were beheaded near here during the Roman persecutions of AD 250 for refusing to abandon their faith (hence the name of the village). A church within the village is dedicated to their memory and a modern chapel just outside is said to contain the martyred saints' tombs. The main road passes the entrance to Gortys (see **A-Z**), the large, sprawling, poorly-marked site of a Greco-Roman city (0800-1900; Moderate; free on Sun.). Continue on the main road towards Mires. Turn left after about 16 km.

63 km – Phaestos (see **A-Z**). The site of a Minoan town built by the same workmen as those who constructed Knossos (see **A-Z**). It boasts the best-preserved palace from the Cretan-Minoan period (0800-1900; Expensive). Take the right fork just past the site's car park and drive for 3 km, stopping at the end of the paved road. Steps lead down to Agia Triada.

66 km – Agia Triada (see **A-Z**). The palace here, which is set in beautiful countryside, is modest in comparison with Phaestos and Knossos, and is believed to have been the summer retreat or residence of a prince (0830-1500; Moderate; free on Sun.). Return to the main road and turn left.

85 km – Agia Galini. This fishing village now has a rapidly-expanding tourist trade but still has much of its old charm. There are interesting caves nearby and numerous tavernas and bars where you can stop for

Agia Galini

refreshments. You'll find inexpensive parking on the quay. There are two small, crowded beaches accessible by a cliff track if you feel like a swim, although the best beaches lie to the west. Leaving the village, return along the road by which you entered for several kilometres, signposted Timbaki and Heraklion, then turn left, signposted Amari, and continue for another few kilometres before forking right and heading inland. Turn right at Apadoulou for Horia after 5 km.

105 km – Kamares. It is possible to climb to the famous Kamares Cave (1520 m), a Minoan sanctuary discovered in 1890, from here but, since the round trip takes nearly 8 hr and the climb is steep, it is not recommended for the casual walker. The cave gave its name to Kamares ware, a fine prehistoric pottery found here. Carry on in the same direction for another 11 km. Turn left and continue for 1 km.

116 km – Moni Vrondisi. A famous 14thC monastery with interesting frescoes and an ornate 15thC Venetian fountain under a shady plane tree. This is a haven of peace and quiet after the road. Return to the main road.

119 km – Zaros. A typical attractive Cretan village with several ancient churches. Continue east and you will eventually reach Agia Varvara, through which you have already passed. From here return to Heraklion along the same route (169 km).

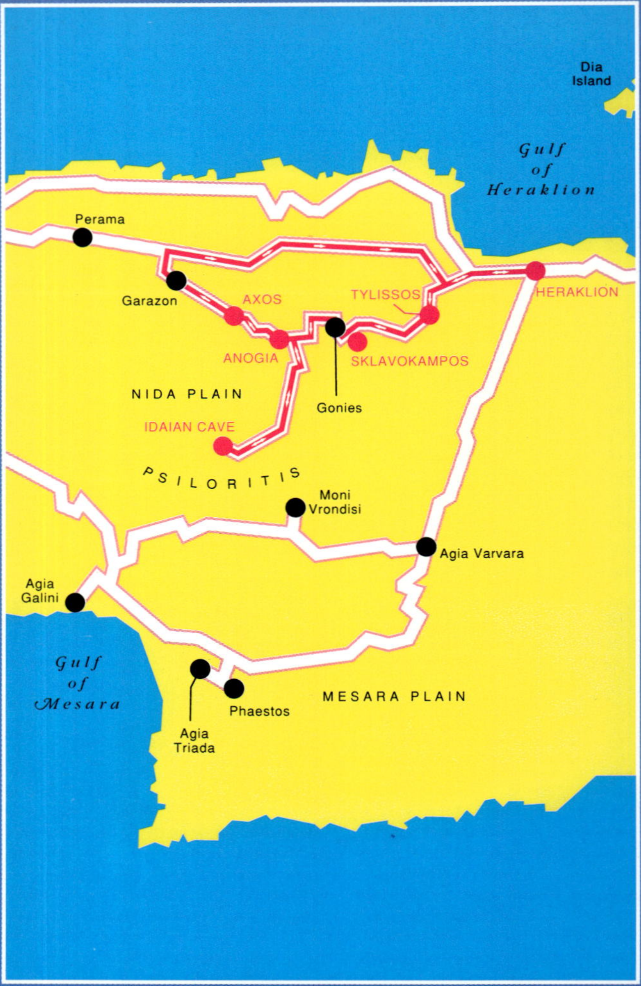

Dia Island
Gulf of Heraklion
Perama
Garazon
AXOS
TYLISSOS
HERAKLION
ANOGIA
SKLAVOKAMPOS
NIDA PLAIN
Gonies
IDAIAN CAVE
PSILORITIS
Moni Vrondisi
Agia Varvara
Agia Galini
Gulf of Mesara
Phaestos
Agia Triada
MESARA PLAIN

Excursion 2

A one-day excursion to Psiloritis (Mount Ida) and the Idaian Cave, taking in the ancient sites of Tylissos, Sklavokampos and Axos, and the picturesque village of Anogia.

Take the westerly road out of Heraklion through the Porta Chania (Chania Gate). Turn left after 10 km and head along the northern slopes of Psiloritis. The road runs through hilly agricultural land with vineyards and olive groves.

15 km – Tylissos. The ruins of three large Minoan villas here, destroyed between 1450 and 1400 BC, constitute one of Crete's earliest and most important archaeological sites (0830-1500; Moderate). Finds from the site are displayed in the Archaeological Museum at Heraklion (see **HERAKLION-ATTRACTIONS**).

20 km – Sklavokampos. Excavations of another Minoan villa. Continue through the village of Gonies. Just before the village of Anogia, turn left and drive up the winding road leading to the Nida Plain, an isolated and desolate area.

56 km – Idaian Cave (see **A-Z**). From the end of the road it is a 20 min walk to the entrance of the cave which, along with the Diktaean Cave (see **A-Z**), is famous in Greek mythology as Zeus' birthplace (see **Myths & Legends**). Return down the same road and turn left onto the main road at Anogia.

76 km – Anogia. The village suffered great damage during World War II. It is notable for its brightly-coloured woven goods and folk traditions (see **Best Buys**, **Ceremonies**, **Crafts**) and is a popular stopping-off point for organized excursions. Continue in a northwesterly direction but beware of rockfalls and potholes.

84 km – Axos. Five minutes' walk beyond the village (signposted) is the site of ancient Axos. Once an important town, there is little to be seen here today, although the Cyclopean walls can still be made out. Finds from the site are housed in Heraklion's Archaeological Museum. Visit the village's Byzantine church to see some superb frescoes (those by Ai Yannis are particularly noteworthy) before heading through Garazon to the old Perama–Heraklion road, where you should turn right to return to the capital (138 km).

PETALO
Heraklion
CLUB ARIA
Chersonisos
Malia
Elounda
Gulf of Mirabello
Vai
Archanes
Neapolis
Kastelli
AKTI
LE FIGARO
GEORGE'S PLACE
Agios Nikolaos
Sitia
ATRIUM
ARIADNI
TAKE FIVE
COTTON CLUB
Zakros
Males
Ano Viannos
Ierapetra
Agii Deka

See **Opening Times**.

COTTON CLUB/ATHENA BAR & DISCO Ikarou Street, Heraklion. Below Eleftherias Square. ● Expensive.
The nightspot for the city's young; bars, live bands, disco.

ARIADNI Knossos Avenue, Heraklion.
5 km south of the city centre just before Knossos. Taxi. ● Expensive.
Atmospheric nightclub with Cretan folk music and dancing (see **A-Z***).*

AKTI Malia. On the seafront. ● Expensive.
Pleasant bar with a relaxed atmosphere and delicious cocktails.

CLUB ARIA Chersonisos.
On the right of the road entering the town. ● Expensive.
Classy-looking disco; one of the best in the area. Theme nights.

TAKE FIVE Off Venizelou Square, Heraklion.
Up from 25 Avgoustou Street. ● Moderate.
Small bar opening onto a park. Interesting cocktails and good music.

ATRIUM Bofor Street, Heraklion.
Up from the harbour bus station. ● Moderate.
Trendy disco with modern décor and lights. Good music.

PETALO Linoperamata.
10 km west of Heraklion, just after cement works. Taxi. ● Moderate.
Big nightclub; bars, food, disco and cabaret. Cretan music and dancing.

LE FIGARO Malia.
At the eastern end of the seafront. ● Moderate.
Modern disco with good lights and waterside cocktail bar.

GEORGE'S PLACE Malia.
On the beach road near the resort. ● Moderate.
Friendly bar popular with Americans from the nearby bases.

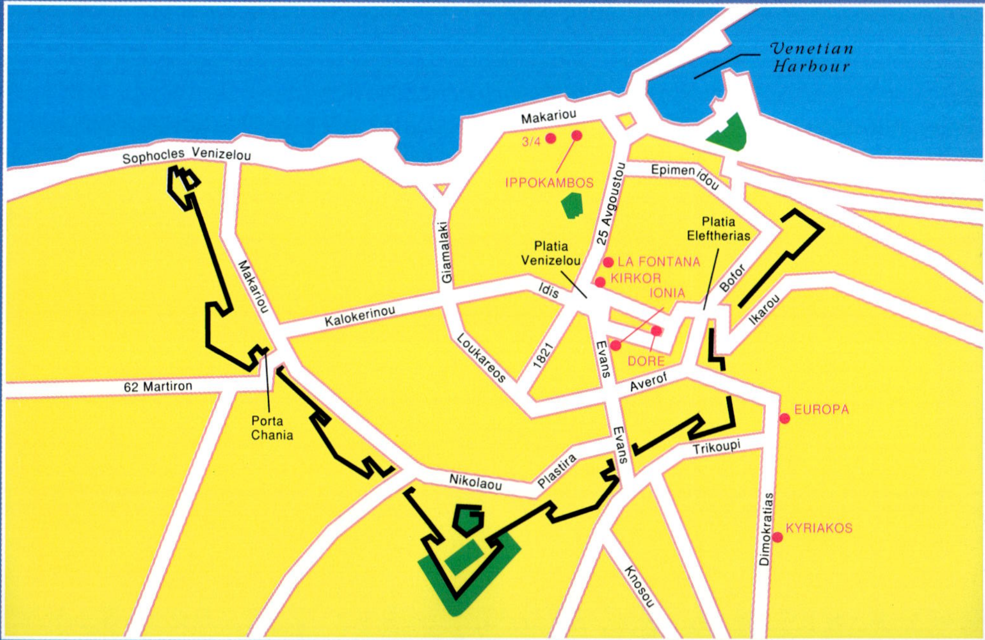
Venetian Harbour
Makariou
3/4
IPPOKAMBOS
Sophocles Venizelou
Epimenidou
25 Avgoustou
Platia Eleftherias
Platia Venizelou
LA FONTANA
KIRKOR
IONIA
Giamalaki
Idis
Bofor
Makariou
Kalokerinou
Ikarou
Loukareos
1821
Evans
DORE
Averof
62 Martiron
Porta Chania
EUROPA
Evans
Trikoupi
Nikolaou
Plastira
Dimokratias
KYRIAKOS
Knosou

KYRIAKOS Dimokratias Avenue 51.
Just outside the city walls. ■ Lunch and evening. ● Expensive.
Elegant restaurant with lots of greenery and very good Greek food.

DORE Eleftherias Square.
Fifth floor and roof terrace; lift in arcade. ■ Lunch and evening.
● Expensive.
Very pleasant in hot weather. Lovely views over the city.

3/4 Makariou Street.
Just beyond the old harbour. ■ Closed in summer. ● Expensive.
Restaurant and piano bar in lovely old building. International cuisine.

IONIA Evans Street 5.
In the town centre. ■ All day. ● Moderate.
Modern taverna/café serving all the usual Cretan dishes.

EUROPA Dimokratias Avenue 9.
Just outside the city walls. ■ Lunch and evening. ● Moderate.
Small, clean, modern restaurant serving simple European cuisine.

LA FONTANA Venizelou Street 24.
Just off Venizelou Square. ■ All day. ● Moderate.
Café with sidewalk tables serving snacks and drinks.

IPPOKAMBOS Mutsotakis Street.
Between the old port and the Xenia Hotel. ■ 1530-1900.
● Inexpensive.
A typical ouzeri *– come here for ouzo and mezedes before dinner.*

KIRKOR Venizelou Square.
By the fountain. ■ All day. ● Inexpensive.
A traditional bougatsa *shop.* Bougatsa *is a hot cheese pastry sprinkled with sugar. A good shady place to watch the passers-by.*

FORTEZZA
Chapel
Cheimaras
ARCHAEOLOGICAL MUSEUM
Salaminos
Venetian Harbour
Melissinou
RIMONDI FOUNTAIN
NERANDZES MOSQUE
Koronaiou Panou
Paraliaki
Nikiforou Foka
Ethnikis Antistaseos
Arkadiou
El. Venizelou
VENETIAN LOGGIA
Dimakopoulou
NTOG
Sofokli Venizelou
Platia Iroon
Giamboudaki
G. Chortazi
Gerakari
Koundourioti
Igoum. Gavriil
PUBLIC GARDENS
AGIOS FRANCISKOS

FORTEZZA (VENETIAN FORTRESS)
Overlooking the city at the western end of the seafront. ▪ 0800-2000. ● Inexpensive.
Impressive ramparts and ruins of the original 16thC stronghold. It is the best vantage point for views of the town and an atmospheric setting for open-air concerts in summer. See **A-Z**.

ARCHAEOLOGICAL MUSEUM At the entrance to the Fortezza.
▪ 0800-1900 Tue.-Sun. ● Moderate; free on Sun.
Local finds from the Neolithic period to Venetian times, including bronzes, jewellery, sculpture and sarcophagi.

VENETIAN LOGGIA Paleologou Street.
Near the old port. ▪ Interior closed to the public.
The town's historic political and commercial meeting place. Impressive 16thC arcaded façade.

RIMONDI FOUNTAIN Petichaki Square.
At the opposite end of Paleologou Street from the old port.
Early-17thC Venetian fountain decorated with columns and lions' heads. See **A-Z**.

NERANDZES MOSQUE Lasthenous Street.
Off Petichaki Square. ▪ 0900-1430 Mon.-Fri.
Old mosque which is now home to a music school. The pretty minaret is currently closed because of damage but concerts are held occasionally in the main hall. You may hear pupils practising.

AGIOS FRANCISKOS Ethnikis Anistaseos Street.
Near the Nerandzes Mosque. ▪ Open for exhibitions 1000-1800.
Venetian church with a richly decorated main door, now restored and open for exhibitions of craftwork and painting.

PUBLIC GARDENS Koundourioti Street. Near the Porta Guora.
Originally an Ottoman graveyard, the gardens are now most notable as the site of the annual wine festival in late July (see **Events***).*

Chania
Kastelli
Platanos
Paleochora
Chora Sfakion
GEORGIOUPOLI
PETRES
RETHYMNON
Rethymnon
PANORAMOS
BALI
Perama
Selia
RODAKINO
PLAKIAS
PREVELI
Spili
Agia Galini

RETHYMNON
In front of the resort.
Long, popular stretch of sand with shallow water safe for swimming.

PETRES 15 km west of Rethymnon.
Chania bus to Episkopi turn-off.
Long, sandy beach extending from the Petres river to Georgioupoli (see below). There are dangerous currents and undertow in places.

GEORGIOUPOLI 27 km west of Rethymnon.
Regular bus service.
Other end of the sandy beach which starts at Petres (see above). Shallow waters at this small, pleasant resort are protected by a breakwater.

RODAKINO 45 km southwest of Rethymnon and 2 km from Rodakino.
Attractive beach of fine sand and pebble surrounded by rocks and caves.

PLAKIAS 39 km southwest of Rethymnon.
Regular bus service.
Long, magnificent but exposed beach stretching between Cape Kakomouri and Cape Stavros at this popular resort.

PREVELI 35 km south of Rethymnon.
Bus to monastery then 20-30 min walk.
Picturesque, palm-fringed beach below the monastery. *See* **RETHYMNON-EXCURSION**.

PANORMOS 24 km east of Rethymnon.
Access from the new road. Car.
Two small beaches – one sandy, one rocky – at this historic village.

BALI 35 km east of Rethymnon.
Access from the new road. Bus then walk.
Three sheltered beaches of sand and pebble set in coves at this attractive little resort at the foot of the mountains.

RETHYMNON
MONI ASOMATON
Amari
Agios
Ioanni
SPILI
Myrthios
Asomatos
PLAKIAS
MONI PREVELI
AGIA
GALINI
Timbaki

A one-day excursion to Moni Preveli, Plakias, Spili and Moni Asomaton.

Take the Spili exit from the new Rethymnon bypass and follow signs for Spili, turning right after 16 km towards Asomatos and Preveli.
22 km – Kourtaliotis Gorge (see **A-Z**). A dramatic drive through a steep-sided limestone ravine but do look out for rockfalls. Turn left in Asomatos (24 km), where Preveli is signposted. Turn left after 2 km.
30 km – Moni Preveli. A spectacularly sited 17thC monastery where Allied soldiers were hidden during World War II before escaping from the beach below. There are several plaques thanking the monks for their help and a small museum. To reach the beach (see **RETHYMNON-BEACHES**) retrace your steps by 4 km to where there is a rough road off to the right. To continue the excursion return to the first junction and turn left, passing through Lefkogio.
42 km – Plakias (see **RETHYMNON-BEACHES**). This small resort has a good beach and is popular for spear fishing. Head for the Bakery Place by the harbour for wonderful fresh pastries and coffee. Return to the main road, turn left through Myrthios and then right, after the gorge, for Agios Ioanni (49 km). When you reach the main road (after 10 km), turn right, again following signs for Spili.
67 km – Spili. A beautiful hillside village with a tree-lined square, springs and a Venetian fountain, traditional houses and Byzantine churches. Keep on the same road for 25 km to Agia Galini (see **HERAKLION-EXCURSION 1**). There is an inexpensive car park on the quay and a choice of tavernas for lunch. Return to the main road and take the road for Timbaki. Turn left after 5 km and drive towards Amari. Turn right at the fork 1.5 km further on, left after another 4 km, then continue straight on.
121 km – Moni Asomaton. This beautiful monastery now houses an agricultural school. Continue northwest towards Rethymnon and enjoy the spectacular passes and side views across rural Crete, dotted with olive groves and villages, tiny white churches and vineyards (152 km).

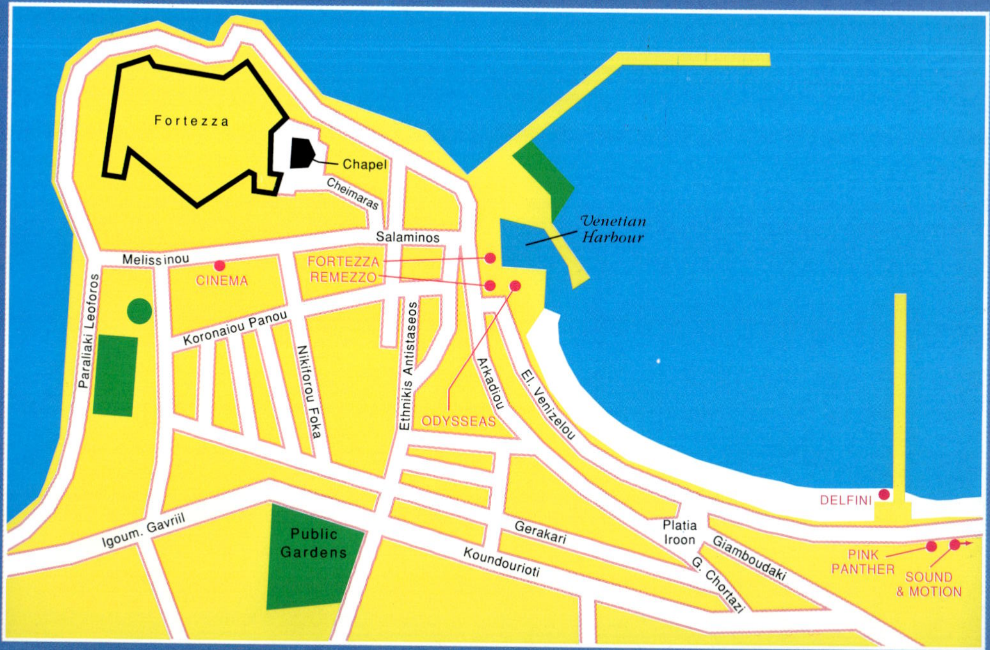
Fortezza
Chapel
Cheimaras
Salaminos
Venetian Harbour
Melissinou
CINEMA
FORTEZZA
REMEZZO
Paraliaki Leoforos
Koronaiou Panou
Nikiforou Foka
Ethnikis Antistaseos
Arkadiou
El. Venizelou
ODYSSEAS
DELFINI
Igoum. Gavriil
Public Gardens
Gerakari
Koundourioti
Platia Iroon
Giamboudaki
G. Chortazi
PINK PANTHER
SOUND & MOTION

Nightlife

See **Opening Times**.

FORTEZZA Old Port
Beside the old inner harbour. ● Expensive.
Air-conditioned disco and bar popular with a young clientele.

CINEMA Melisinou.
Below the Venetian fortress. ● Expensive.
The *place to go. A disco in a converted cinema building, which is huge and busy.*

PINK PANTHER Sofokli Venizelou Street 42.
On the seafront near the Kriti Beach Hotel. ● Moderate.
Small, modern cocktail bar facing the sea; also serves snacks.

REMEZZO Ioulias Petichaki Street 8.
Beside the old inner harbour. ● Moderate.
Popular but small bar with good music and dancing.

DELFINI Sofokli Venizelou Street.
On the seafront. ● Moderate.
Large steakhouse and open-air disco on the beach with banana trees and good lighting.

ODYSSEAS Old Port.
Additional entrance off Ioulias Petichaki Street. ● Moderate.
Tarted up taverna with bouzouki and Greek dancing, as well as food and a bar.

SOUND & MOTION Sofokli Venizelou Street.
Behind the beach 1 km east of the town. ● Moderate.
Modern disco with a good atmosphere, and a relaxed bar with seating on the seafront.

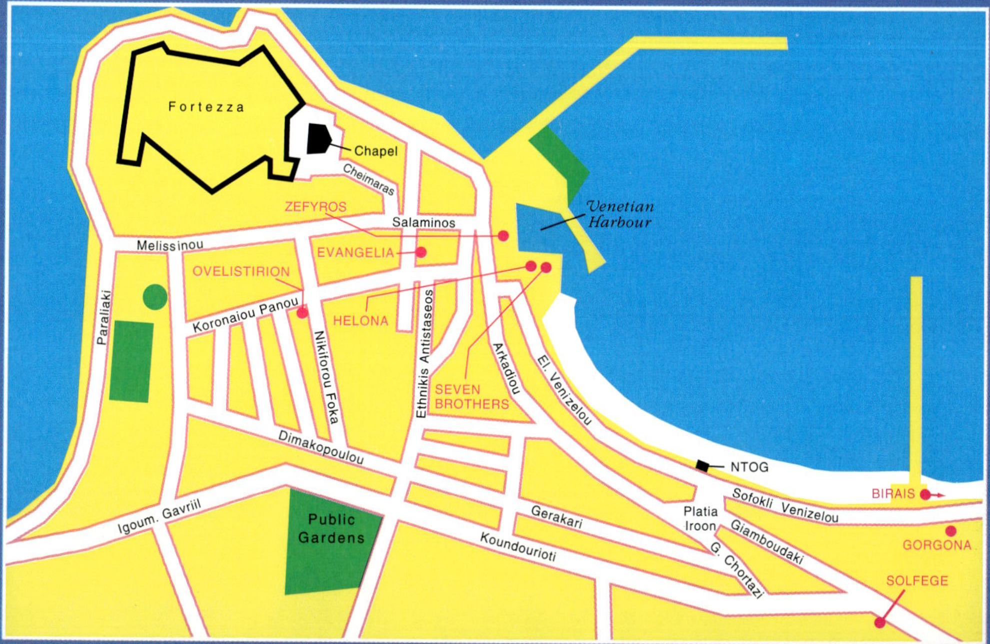

Fortezza
Chapel
Cheimaras
ZEFYROS
Salaminos
Venetian Harbour
Melissinou
EVANGELIA
OVELISTIRION
Koronaiou Panou
HELONA
Nikiforou Foka
Ethnikis Antistaseos
Paraliaki
SEVEN BROTHERS
Arkadiou
El. Venizelou
Dimakopoulou
NTOG
BIRAIS
Sofokli Venizelou
Platia Iroon
Giamboudaki
Gerakari
Koundourioti
G. Chortazi
Igoum. Gavriil
Public Gardens
GORGONA
SOLFEGE

GORGONA Papanastasiou Street.
Corner of Sofokli Venizelou Street, next door to the Kriti Beach Hotel.
▪ 1100-0200. ● Expensive.
European menu as well as local fish dishes. Large and dependable.

HELONA Old Port.
▪ Mid-morning until late. ● Expensive.
Tables beside the old harbour. Seafood a speciality.

SEVEN BROTHERS Old Port.
▪ Lunch and evening. ● Expensive.
Another tourist trap but the setting is attractive and the food good.

SOLFEGE Koundourioti Street 153.
On the main street in the town centre. ▪ Evening. ● Expensive.
Big restaurant/bar with a European menu, live piano and bouzouki music.

BIRAIS Sofokli Venizelou Street 62-63.
On the seafront. ▪ All day. ● Moderate.
Modern taverna serving all the usual dishes. Lively and informal.

OVELISTIRION Nikiforou Foka Street 98.
Opposite the church of the Annunciation. ▪ All day. ● Moderate.
Modest taverna opening onto a quiet square and offering the usual range of traditional dishes.

ZEFYROS Old Port.
▪ Lunch and evening. ● Moderate.
Less aggressive than some establishments round here. Typical Cretan cuisine but no shade.

EVANGELIA Diogeni-Moskoviti Street 6.
Behind the Rimondi Fountain. ▪ All day. ● Moderate.
Charming shady café serving good fruit juices, coffee and snacks.

FORTEZZA
Cheimaras
CHURCH OF ST. ANTHONY
Salaminos
ARCHAEOLOGICAL MUSEUM
RIMONDI FOUNTAIN
Theod. Arambatzoglon
Paleologou
NERANDZES MOSQUE
Lasthenous
CHURCH OF THE ANNUNCIATION
Nikiforou Foka
Ethnikis Antistaseos
VENETIAN LOGGIA
Venetian Harbour
El. Venizelou
Arkadiou
AGIOS FRANCISKOS
Platia Petichaki
PORTA GUORA
MINARET
NTOG
Public Gardens
KARA PASHA MOSQUE
Gerakari
Koundourioti
CHURCH OF THE FOUR MARTYRS
Platia Iroon

Walk

Duration: 1 hr-1 hr 30 min.

Start at the seafront near the NTOG office (see **Tourist Information**). Cross Iroon Square and turn into Victor Ougo Street, on the corner of which stands the Kara Pasha mosque, looking rather forlorn in its neglected garden. Just round the corner is one of the city's several Turkish fountains. Take a right turn into Gerakari Street and keep going until you reach a large, modern square. The church of the Four Martyrs is on the left and a graceful minaret can be seen to the right above the rooftops of the surrounding houses. Enter the old city through the Porta Guora, one of the few surviving parts of the original city walls, and continue down Ethnikis Antistaseos Street to Agios Franciskos (see **RETHYMNON-ATTRACTIONS**), with its partially restored façade, down a side passage to the left. At the end of the passage stands the imposing gateway of the Turkish school which still functions as a primary school. Continue along Ethnikis Antistaseos Street and before you enter Petichaki Square turn left into Lasthenous Street, which leads to the Nerandzes mosque (see **RETHYMNON-ATTRACTIONS**). Lasthenous and the surrounding streets are typical of the older quarter where Venetian doorways and arches exist cheek by jowl with wooden Turkish balconies, and modern dwellings stand next to the empty shells of Venetian houses. Turn right into Nikiforou Foka Street at the top of Lasthenous Street and you will come to a quiet little square containing the Venetian church of the Annunciation. Turn right down Theod. Arambatzoglon Street and follow it back to Petichaki Square, where water still flows from the three lions' head faucets of the Rimondi Fountain (see **RETHYMNON-ATTRACTIONS, A-Z**). Continue down Paleologou Street, passing the Venetian Loggia (see **RETHYMNON-ATTRACTIONS**), and the adjoining Nearchou Street going towards the harbour. You are now in the lively area of the Venetian harbour with its numerous restaurants and discos. Turn left at the end of the harbour into Salaminos Street, passing the Catholic church of St. Anthony on the right. Take a diagonal right turn down Cheimaras Street which leads to the huge Fortezza (see **RETHYMNON-ATTRACTIONS, A-Z**) that dominates the town. The Archaeological Museum (see **RETHYMNON-ATTRACTIONS**) is now housed in a restored bastion opposite the entrance.

Agia Ekaterini, Heraklion: The church was formerly a monastic school and, in the 16th-17thC, a centre of Cretan art, theology, literature and culture. It is now a Museum of Religious Art containing six superb 16thC icons by the great Cretan painter, Damiskinos. See HERAKLION-ATTRACTIONS.

Agia Galini: See HERAKLION-EXCURSION 1.

Agia Triada: Built c. 1600 BC, the palace consists of two perpendicular wings and is believed to have been either a royal retreat from Phaestos (see **A-Z**) or the residence of a prince. Some of the finest examples of Minoan art have been found here, including frescoes, a painted sarcophagus and three famous vases of black soapstone (the Harvester Vase, the Boxer Vase and the Chieftain Cup), which are now on display in Heraklion's Archaeological Museum (see HERAKLION-ATTRACTIONS, **A-Z**). See HERAKLION-EXCURSION 1.

Agios Nikolaos: Pop: 20,000. 70 km southeast of Heraklion. The capital of Lasithi. Beautifully situated on the gulf of Mirabello, the town enjoys a mild, dry climate and a booming tourist industry. The attractive town centre is enhanced by a freshwater lake which is now joined to the outer port by an artificial channel and serves as an inner harbour. A small museum to the northwest contains many finds from excavations in the Lasithi province (0845-1500 Wed.-Mon.; Moderate). Visitors can enjoy the numerous restaurants, tavernas and cafés around the seafront, lake and harbour areas, as well as the rather busy beaches both in and near the town. Boats leave the harbour for other islands such as Karpathos. See AGIOS NIKOLAOS.

Amnisos: 7 km east of Heraklion. This was the principal port serving Knossos (see **A-Z**) during the Minoan period and excavations have revealed a villa and shrine dating from that time. The famous Frescoes of the Lilies (c. 1600 BC) found on the site are housed in the Heraklion Archaeological Museum (see HERAKLION-ATTRACTIONS, **A-Z**). The beach here, which has plenty of tavernas and cafés nearby, is one of the capital's closest and can be reached by Bus 1 from the city.

Agios Nikolaos

Aptera: 15 km east of Chania. The ruins of an ancient city with magnificent views over Soudha bay. It survived into the early Christian era before being plundered by Arab pirates. A monastery, enclosed by the city walls, marks the centre of the site, which includes a classical Greek temple and theatre, underground arched cisterns and a Byzantine temple. The Turkish fortress of Izzedin, standing on the outskirts, guarded the entrance to Soudha harbour. 0800-1500; Free.

Archaeological Museum, Chania: Housed in the church of Agios Francisko, once one of Crete's finest churches, the museum displays finds from the excavations at Aptera (see **A-Z**) and Polyrrina (see **A-Z**). The range of exhibits dates back to Neolithic times and includes inscribed tablets, Minoan seals and pottery, Greek and Roman glassware, classical sculptures and mosaics. See **CHANIA-ATTRACTIONS**.

Archaeological Museum, Heraklion: One of the world's finest archaeological museums traces Crete's ancient past up to Roman times and houses some splendid Minoan treasures. The rooms are well laid out in chronological and geographical order. The following exhibits should not be missed:

Room 3 – Fine Kamares ceramics (see **HERAKLION-EXCURSION 1**); the Phaestos Disk with its undeciphered hieroglyphics (see **HERAKLION-EXCURSION 1**).
Room 4 – The famous representations of the Snake Goddess from Knossos (see **A-Z**); the sacred Bull's Head vessel of black stone encrusted with rock crystal and mother-of-pearl; a beautifully made games board; a giant royal sword from Malia (see **A-Z**).
Room 7 – Three stone vases and gold jewellery from Agia Triada (see **HERAKLION-EXCURSION 1**, **A-Z**).
Room 8 – A beautiful rock crystal vase from Zakros (see **A-Z**), found in 300 pieces and painstakingly reconstructed.
Room 13 – A wooden model of the palace of Knossos.
Room 14 – Reconstructed Minoan frescoes, including the Prince of Lilies and La Parisienne from Knossos, and the Red and White Lilies from Amnisos (see **A-Z**). A sarcophagus (1400 BC) from Agia Triada (see **A-Z**) dominates the centre of the room.
See **HERAKLION-ATTRACTIONS**.

Caves: There are numerous caves on Crete, because of its limestone formation, which are all linked in some way to the life and history of the islanders. Some, such as those at Matala, have been used as shelters while others, for example at Amnisos, were ancient centres of worship, and still more were places of refuge from the Turks: for instance, the ones at Milatos and Melidoni. Around 300 have been excavated so far and have yielded a wealth of archaeological remains. If you wish to visit any of the caves, check beforehand that they are not under excavation as this may mean that they have been fenced off at the entrance. If, however, the cave you want to visit is open, then go properly equipped with torches, warm clothing and good footwear. See **Diktaean Cave**, **Eileithia Cave**, **Idaian Cave**, **Melidoni Cave**, **Sendoni Cave**.

Ceremonies: A traditional marriage is one of the most colourful ceremonies in Crete. In former days the whole village helped the young couple begin their life together by building their house, cutting the wood to cook their first meal and warm them through their first winter,

and baking and decorating the *koularia* (wedding cakes). On the day of the wedding, baskets of provisions are taken as gifts to the new house, and at midday the dowry is taken to the bridegroom's house in a procession led by a lyre player. After the ceremony, which includes the symbolic exchange of crowns, the villagers pin banknotes to the bride's dress and the parents hang gold coins round her neck. Two knives placed at the entrance to the new house are intended to chase away evil spirits, and the bride throws in a few grains of grenadine to ensure future happiness. You can still see traditional weddings at the village of Anogia (see **HERAKLION-EXCURSION 2**) and the ceremony is laid on for tourists in late Aug. at Kritsa (see **AGIOS NIKOLAOS-ATTRACTIONS, A-Z**). See **Customs**.

Chania: Pop: 60,000. 165 km west of Heraklion. The capital of the province of Chania and the former capital of the island. Chania is a beautiful town of great historical interest. It was built on the ruins of the ancient city of Kydonia. During World War II it suffered heavy bombardment which destroyed virtually all of the town apart from the area around the old port where you can still see examples of Venetian and Turkish architecture in the quarters known as Splanzia and Kastelli. The old town also has a large number of leather shops selling bags, sandals and boots. The new town boasts a splendid municipal market building, constructed in the form of a cross, which is supposedly modelled on the market at Marseille. The Historical Museum & Archives, to the southeast of the town, contains an interesting collection of Turkish and Venetian manuscripts, and the Municipal Gardens have a tiny zoo, children's playground, café and auditorium. This last is used as an open-air cinema and venue for folk displays and cultural performances: contact the NTOG office for details (see **Tourist Information**). See **CHANIA**.

Chersonisos: 29 km east of Heraklion. The small port of Limin Chersonisos, to give it its full and proper title, has become one of the largest tourist centres on Crete, with hotels, restaurants and beaches spreading for miles along the coast. However, some of the charm remains in spite of the influx of visitors. The port flourished during the Roman and Byzantine periods and you can see submerged Roman ruins along the shoreline. The old village of Chersonisos lies 2 km inland. See **HERAKLION-BEACHES**.

Crafts: Weaving is a major form of Cretan popular art involving techniques which are handed down from mother to daughter, with each weaver adding her own personal touch to the age-old designs. All the materials used – wool, cotton, linen and silk, and vegetable dyes – are home-produced. Traditionally, when Cretan men chose a bride, her skill in weaving was regarded as of the upmost importance. See **Best Buys**.

Dia Island: 12 km northeast of Heraklion. A small, rocky islet which is one of three sanctuaries for the long-horned wild goats known as *kri-kri*. The little church of Analipsi hosts a saint's day feast (see **Festivities**) in June and there is a taverna which opens in summer when there are regular boat services to the island.

Diktaean Cave: The mythical birthplace of Zeus (see **Myths & Legends**) situated above the Lasithi plateau near Psychro. Excavations began here in the late 19thC and have yielded rich finds. There is evidence that the cave was used as a centre of cult worship in the Minoan period. The interior has impressive stalactites and stalagmites. Visitors to the cave are recommended to take suitable non-slip footwear and a torch, though candles are available for 100 Drs. See **AGIOS NIKOLAOS-EXCURSION 2**, **Caves**.

Eileithia Cave: 1 km from Amnisos. This cave was consecrated to I ithya, the goddess of childbirth, and was an important shrine of cult worship from Neolithic to Roman times. You can reach it on Bus 1 from Heraklion. See **Caves**.

El Greco (1541-1614): The great Greek painter Domenikos Theotokopoulos was born on Crete, possibly in the town of Fodele (see **A-Z**) but more likely in Heraklion. He left the island as a young man and acquired his artistic reputation after working and studying in Italy and Spain, but was in the habit of appending Kres, or Cretan, to his name.

Elyros: 67 km southwest of Chania. One of two ancient sites near the town of Sougia. This Doric settlement possesses the ruins of a theatre, an aqueduct and a church. To get to it take the Sougia bus from Kydonias Street, Chania and then be prepared for a 1 hr walk. Admission is free. See **Lissos**.

Evans, Sir Arthur John (1851-1941): The English archaeologist and former curator of the Ashmolean Museum responsible for the excavations and reconstruction at Knossos (see **A-Z**) in the first half of this century. This resulted in his discovery of a pre-Phoenician script and a separate and distinct Bronze-Age civilization he called Minoan. One of his most famous publications was entitled *The Palace of Minos at Knossos*.

Festivities: The main festivities on the island occur on the feast days of the local patron saints. The *panegyria*, as it is called, really begins in each village on the eve of the feast day, when everyone from the surrounding countryside gathers to spend the night singing and dancing.

The celebrations then begin all over again after Mass the following day. Traditionally, visitors who come to experience the festivities are made welcome guests of the village and are offered hospitality in every house (see **Customs**). Needless to say, with growing numbers of tourists flocking to the villages to see the celebrations, it is not practicable for the local people to honour this tradition today, although you may still get a taste of it in remoter villages during the low season. See **Ceremonies**, **Events**.

Fodele: 22 km east of Heraklion. A picturesque village in attractive countryside. Once considered to be the birthplace of El Greco (see **A-Z**), there are various memorials honouring him here. You can reach the village by bus from Heraklion's Porta Chania.

Folk Dancing: Typical Cretan folk dancing takes the form of a chain, with the dancers holding each other by the hand or shoulder. Unlike many Greek dances, everyone dances, not just the leaders of the chain. All the dances are accompanied by at least one musician and singing. The following dances are the most common:
Kastrinos – A slow, rhythmic dance with small steps, which comes from Heraklion.
Pendozalis – A fast, spirited dance popular all over Crete, which was made famous in the film *Zorba the Greek*.
Sousta – An erotic, improvised dance for two, originating in Rethymnon, which demands a certain degree of grace, suppleness and imagination.
Syrtos – A circle dance in which the leader sometimes performs spectacular routines.

Folk Music: The origins of Cretan music would appear be rooted in early Minoan culture. Cretan songs are characterized by a rich expressiveness, yet they are also tender. Although a limited range of notes is used, the music is normally lively and the melody forceful. The two basic types of folk song are *mandinades*, a living form reflecting the traditional character of the Cretan people and tending to deal with universal subjects such as love and death, and *rizitika*, songs of the White

Mountains with somewhat sentimental heroic or patriotic themes which constitute a fairly sophisticated form of Cretan popular poetry (usually accompanied by the bouzouki).
The main musical instrument in Crete is the lyre (*lyra*) which is derived from the smaller *lyriki*. Other traditional instruments include the *laouto* (a type of mandolin), the *askomantoura* (resembling bagpipes), and the *habioli* or shepherd's flute. The bouzouki, brought from the Orient by refugees in the 1920s, is popular all over Greece. It was banned for a while by the government but is now experiencing a revival among modern Greek composers.

Fortezza, Rethymnon: This massive fort was built in the 16thC by the Venetians in order to protect the town from raiding pirates. Maps from that period show that the structure originally contained barracks, a military governor's residence, a hospital and arsenals. Despite its strategic position, the fort fell to the Turks in the middle of the 17thC. The ramparts, however, are especially well preserved and offer good views over the town and coastline. The centre is dominated by the large domed mosque of Ibrahim Han. Concerts and drama are staged within the walls in summer. See RETHYMNON-ATTRACTIONS.

Frangokastello: The fortress of Frangokastello to the east of Chora Sfakion was built in 1371 as a defence against pirates as well as to maintain order among the local inhabitants. In 1828 Greek rebels occupied the fortress and were subsequently massacred by Turkish invaders. Under certain climatic conditions atmospheric shapes occur which, it is claimed, represent the ghosts of the defeated army. The castle is now largely a ruin and the beach (see CHANIA-BEACHES) is one of the most beautiful on the island. However, it can get very windy here.

Gaidhouronisi (Hrisi) Islet: There are day excursions by fishing boat (takes 1 hr) from Ierapetra to this tiny (1 km long), deserted island with its beautiful sandy beaches.

Gavdos Island: A large island 50 km off Paleochora on the south coast (boats run from Paleochora and Chora Sfakion), with a population of less than 100. Although it is a barren and inhospitable place, the island does possess magnificent beaches. There is a port at Karabo, an inland capital called Kastri, and two other small settlements at Vatsiana (south of Kastri) and Ambelos (to the north), both of which have marvellous beaches. There is no mains electricity, limited supplies of fresh water and only a few vehicles on the island, so be prepared to walk. Food supplies are also limited as the island depends, to a large extent, on imported goods.

Gortys: 46 km southwest of Heraklion. This site, now occupied by the remains of a large Greco-Roman city, was inhabited as early as Minoan times but flourished under Dorian rule. The most fascinating discovery from the site is a series of stone tablets dating from the 5thC BC inscribed with the Law Code of Gortyn. This describes, in Dorian-Greek dialect (running from left to right, then right to left, and so on), the penalties for certain crimes as well as legislation on civil matters. After the period of Dorian rule Gortys continued to prosper under the Romans and most of the remains are from that era, including an odeon

Gortys

(part of which was built with Law Code stones), a sanctuary and an amphitheatre. You can also see the remains of a large 7thC church, the basilica of Agios Titus (see **St. Titus**). The Byzantine city of Gortys was finally destroyed by Arab raiders in AD 824 after already suffering the effects of catastrophic earthquakes. See **HERAKLION-EXCURSION 1.**

Gournia: 19 km southeast of Agios Nikolaos. This extremely well-preserved Minoan town reached the peak of its prosperity during the middle-Minoan period. Outstanding among the many remaining buildings are the small Palace of the Overlord and the public courtyard or marketplace. The wide variety of finds, now housed in the Archaeological Museum of Heraklion (see **HERAKLION-ATTRACTIONS**, **A-Z**), supports the theory that Gournia was once a wealthy and important centre. See **AGIOS NIKOLAOS-ATTRACTIONS.**

Heraklion: Pop: 150,000. The commercial and political capital of Crete and the fifth-largest city in Greece. The old city of Heraklion and its chief tourist attractions (the harbour, museums, churches and monuments) lie within the 5 km-long, 15thC Venetian walls with their four gates and seven bastions. Much of the city's commercial activity occurs in the modern part of town beyond the old walls, while the port supports a constant sea traffic with the mainland and other islands (see **Ferries**). An airport just outside the capital handles both international and inter-island flights (see **Airports**). Heraklion also boasts a bustling nightlife with a variety of restaurants and discos. See **HERAKLION.**

Historical & Ethnographical Museum, Heraklion: The museum houses a wide variety of displays tracing the history and culture of the island from the period when Knossos (see **A-Z**) flourished as its capital up to the present day, including the Byzantine, Venetian and Turkish eras. Exhibits include sculpture, inscribed tablets, religious objects, carvings, icons, flags and arms. There is also a vaulted chapel decorated with 15thC frescoes, the reconstructed study of the writer Nikos Kazantzakis (see **A-Z**), and the replicated interior of a traditional Cretan home, plus some fine examples of Cretan craftwork (see **Crafts**). See **HERAKLION-ATTRACTIONS.**

Heraklion

Idaian Cave: Another cave associated with Zeus (see **Myths & Legends**). Situated in the Psiloritis Mountains, it has proved to be a rich source of archaeological finds which have provided evidence that the cave was once used as a shrine or centre of worship. It consists of a long, winding passage leading to various inner chambers. Excavations are still under way and access to the interior is currently restricted. See **HERAKLION-EXCURSION 2**, **Caves**.

Ierapetra: Pop: 12,000. 36 km south of Agios Nikolaos. The largest town in the province of Lasithi. Ierapetra is now a largely modern development, although the remains of a Roman theatre can still be seen at the entrance to the town on the Viannos road, a Venetian fortress overlooks the harbour and there is a mosque dating from the Turkish occupation. The town's numerous hotels, restaurants and discos testify to its role as a major tourist resort. See **AGIOS NIKOLAOS-BEACHES, EXCURSION 1**.

Kamares Cave: See **HERAKLION-EXCURSION 1**, **Caves**.

Kazantzakis, Nikos (1885-1957): One of Greece's greatest writers was born in Heraklion. As a boy he was greatly influenced by the 1897 revolution and later went to study in France. A profound socialist, his best-known works include *Freedom or Death*, *Alexis Zorbas* and *Christ Recrucified*. Another of his books, *The Last Temptation*, has been made into a film by Scorsese which has caused much controversy, though this would be nothing new for Kazantzakis who was constantly at loggerheads with the Church because of his religious opinions (he was eventually excommunicated, died in exile and was refused a Catholic burial). He was buried in Heraklion, where you can visit his tomb with its famous inscription (see **HERAKLION-ATTRACTIONS**), and a room devoted to him in the city's Historical & Ethnographical Museum (see **HERAKLION-ATTRACTIONS**, **A-Z**).

Knossos: The reconstructed palace at Knossos, the capital of the Minoan kingdom, is the most famous and impressive archaeological site on Crete. According to legend, King Minos created the labyrinth

Knossos

near here to hide the Minotaur (see **Myths & Legends**). The palace was erected in 1400 BC and discovered by Arthur Evans (see **A-Z**) in 1880. He devoted 43 years of his life to excavating it and his reconstruction has always aroused controversy since much of it was based on speculation. The maze of rooms, many of which have fabulous frescoes, is built round a central courtyard, and there is a sophisticated water and drainage system.

The main features include the central court, the queen's chambers, the throne room and the grand staircase, an excellent piece of design allowing light into the lower storeys of the palace.

To get the most out of a visit to Knossos, splash out and buy one of the detailed, but rather expensive, guidebooks available in shops in the capital. Finds from the site are exhibited in Heraklion's Archaeological Museum (see **HERAKLION-ATTRACTIONS**, **A-Z**). 0800-1900; Expensive. Bus 2 from Heraklion city centre every 20 min.

Lasithi Plateau

Kournas Lake: Crete's only freshwater lake lies 10 km southwest of Georgioupolis and can be reached either by car, or by bus to Georgioupolis and then taxi. It offers a pleasant contrast to the more dramatic scenery of the rest of the island and is home to many birds and animals, including birds of prey.

Kourtaliotis Gorge: 22 km south of Rethymnon. This wild, narrow, 2000 m-long gorge, with its several caves and springs, starts at the village of Koxares. You can reach it by taking the Plakias bus from Rethymnon and getting off at the stop for Kourtaliotis. Steps down from the road lead to the entrance. See **RETHYMNON-EXCURSION**.

Kritsa: 11 km southwest of Agios Nikolaos. This picturesque village is one of the island's largest and is famous for weaving (see **Best Buys**, **Crafts**), delicious locally-produced honey and magnificent views of the valley. Many of the people of Kritsa still wear traditional costumes. The Byzantine church of Panagia Kera, 1 km outside the village, has three naves and is decorated throughout with well-preserved 14th-15thC frescoes. See **AGIOS NIKOLAOS-ATTRACTIONS**, **Ceremonies**.

Lasithi Plateau: The fertile plain of Lasithi, at a height of over 800 m and approximately 10 km by 6 km, is covered by a patchwork of cultivated fields (irrigated by numerous windmills) and is surrounded by the impressive Dikti Mountains (site of the famous Diktaean Cave – see **A-Z**). Villages situated around the edge of the plateau are connected by a circular road. See **AGIOS NIKOLAOS-EXCURSION 2**.

Leben: 80 km southwest of Heraklion. An ancient hill-top sanctuary and spa, dating from the 3rdC BC, once well known for its therapeutic spring waters. Situated just to the east of the seaside village of Lendas, the site can be reached twice daily by bus from Heraklion.

Lissos: 67 km southwest of Chania. One of two ancient sites near the town of Sougia. This settlement has the ruins of a temple and cliff carvings. To get to it take the Sougia bus from Kydonias Street, Chania, and then be prepared for a 1 hr walk. Admission is free. See **Elyros**.

Malia Palace: 4 km from Malia town (see **HERAKLION-BEACHES**) and attractively situated overlooking the sea, the palace is less impressive than either Knossos (see **A-Z**) or Phaestos (see **A-Z**) but has a great many remains dating from 1700-1450 BC, including the ruins of courtyards, royal apartments, halls, corridors, storage areas, pillars, loggia, staircases, altars and a sacrificial pit. The palace was destroyed in 1700 BC and was reconstructed at a later date. Bus from Heraklion harbour. Admission charges are Moderate.

Melidoni Cave: 25 km east of Rethymnon and 4 km northeast of Perama. This stalactite cave can be reached either by car or taxi, or by a 1-2 hr walk from the village. It is a memorial to over 300 villagers who sheltered here in 1824 from the Turkish forces and were asphyxiated by fires lit at the cave entrance to smoke them out. See **Caves**.

Mohlos Island: There are boat excursions from Agios Nikolaos to this tiny island in the gulf of Mirabello. It is an ideal place for bathing and there are Minoan tombs and submerged ruins, as well as tavernas. See **AGIOS NIKOLAOS-EXCURSION 1**.

Monasteries: There were 376 monasteries (*moni*) and nearly 10,000 monks on Crete during Venetian times. Under both Venetian and Turkish rule, the monasteries enjoyed special concessions and so became places of refuge for many Cretans. They also flourished as intellectual and artistic centres, allowing the development of the famous Cretan School which produced artists such as El Greco (see **A-Z**) and Damaskinos. During the Turkish occupation the monasteries were ideal bases for insurrection, being enclosed by walls with towers, furnished with back exits and situated in beautiful, serene spots that also provided their inhabitants with natural defences. Visitors are requested to dress and behave with respect for the monasteries' function as places of worship. Admission to monasteries is free but it is polite to make a donation.

Moni Agia Triada: 16 km northeast of Chania. A renowned early-17thC monastery which was founded by the converted Venetian family of Tzangarola (the Venetian influence is apparent in its architecture). The main attractions include the courtyard and some interesting icons. You can reach the monastery by bus from Chania.

Moni Angarathos: 24 km south of Heraklion. A 16thC monastery which was a seat of great learning during the Cretan renaissance. It also played an important role in the Turkish-Venetian war of the 17thC. The courtyards are particularly attractive.

Moni Arkadi: 20 km southeast of Rethymnon. Situated in beautiful countryside, this 16thC monastery became famous as a symbol of Cretan liberty. In 1866 the monastery sheltered numerous Cretans who were involved in the island's resistance to Turkish occupation. Overwhelmed by the besieging forces, the abbot is said to have decided to blow up the garrison rather than surrender, and gave the order to ignite the ammunition store, causing hundreds of casualties on both sides. The event is commemorated each year in Nov. (see **Events**). During the process of restoration a variety of architectural styles from different periods have been revealed. There is a regular bus service from Rethymnon to the monastery. 0800-1900.

Moni Asomaton: See **RETHYMNON-EXCURSION**.

Moni Gonia: 23 km west of Chania. This 17thC Venetian monastery at Kolimbari houses a collection of fine icons and precious objects. You can reach the monastery by car, or by bus from Kydonias Street in Chania (get off at Kastelli, then walk for 2 km). Closed 1300-1530.

Moni Preveli: See **RETHYMNON-EXCURSION**.

Moni Toplou: An isolated 17thC monastery, resembling a fortress, which sits on a plateau surrounded by hills at the eastern end of Crete. It has traditionally been associated with the defence of Cretan liberty, and was also reputed to possess great wealth. A stone to the left of the entrance to the church is inscribed with a 2ndC BC treaty between Egypt and the Cretan towns of Itanos and Iierapytna (Ierapetra). Inside are some beautiful icons, the most important of which is *Lord Thou Art Great* by Ioannis Kornaros (1770). See **AGIOS NIKOLAOS-EXCURSION 1**.

Moni Vrondisi: See **HERAKLION-EXCURSION 1**.

Myths & Legends: Zeus, supreme ruler of the gods, was hidden in a cave on Crete at his birth to escape being killed by his father, Kronos, who was fearful of being overthrown. The Diktaean Cave (see **AGIOS NIKOLAOS-EXCURSION 1**, **A-Z**) and the Idaian Cave (see **HERAKLION-EXCURSION 2**, **A-Z**) are most associated with legends concerning Zeus, who went on to abduct the Princess Europa from Phoenicia and carry her to Crete where she bore three sons, one of whom was Minos, who eventually became king of the island and founded the Minoan dynasty which held sway over most of the Greek islands and many parts of the mainland. King Minos' wife Pasiphae, having fallen in love with a bull, gave birth to Asterius, commonly known as the Minotaur, the monster endowed with the head of a bull and the body of a man. The creature was condemned to be hidden from sight, imprisoned in the Labyrinth near Knossos (see **A-Z**), which Minos ordered to be constructed by Daedalus. The king then imposed a tribute on Athens, forcing the city to send seven maidens and seven boys, every seven years, to be sacrificed to the Minotaur. This continued until Theseus arrived, voluntarily, on the island as one of the fated fourteen. Ariadne, King Minos' daughter, fell in love with Theseus and, on Daedalus' suggestion, she gave him a sword and a ball of thread, enabling him to kill the Minotaur and escape from the Labyrinth. Daedalus was banished to his own labyrinth for betraying King Minos and helping in the escape plot, and his son Icarus was forced to join him. Daedalus, always the ingenious inventor, then constructed wax and feather wings with which the two could effect their escape from the island. Before their flight the father warned his son from flying either too close to the sea, and wetting his feathers, or too near the sun, which would melt the wax. Forgetting his instructions, Icarus flew too high and fell to his death in the sea now known as the Icarian Sea. Theseus abandoned Ariadne on the island of Naxos and returned to Athens alone.

Moni Preveli

Rethymnon

Paleochora: See CHANIA-BEACHES, EXCURSION.

Phaestos: The second most important centre of Minoan civilization occupies a magnificent site only 5 km from the Libyan Sea, with views of the mountains and the Mesara Plain. The palace was first excavated by an Italian, Federico Halbharr, at the beginning of this century. In contrast to Knossos (see **A-Z**), very little reconstruction work has been carried out. The ruins largely consist of the remains of a palace which was inhabited up to c. 1450 BC. A second palace was built on the foundations of the original structure, and sections of its floor plan are still evident. The site comprises a central courtyard, staterooms, royal quarters, servants' quarters, storerooms and a theatre. Finds from the area, including pottery, jewellery and the undeciphered Phaestos Disk, are displayed in the Archaeological Museum at Heraklion (see HERAKLION-ATTRACTIONS, **A-Z**). See HERAKLION-EXCURSION 1.

Polyrrina: 49 km west of Chania. Ruins of a city dating from the Roman and Byzantine eras. The Cyclopean walls can be traced back to the time of Homer and the aqueduct to the time of Hadrian. There are magnificent views down to the coast.

Rethymnon: Pop: 30,000. The capital of the province of Rethymnon and the third-largest town on the island. Rethymnon is a pleasant place to visit, with its relatively slow pace of life, its long, sandy beach and its huge Venetian Fortezza (see **A-Z**). The old town is particularly attractive and consists of a maze of tiny streets, an inner harbour which can only be used by small vessels, and aristocratic residences decorated by distinctive arches and fine stone stairways. Traditionally a cultural and intellectual centre, and housing several departments of the university of Crete, the town has produced leading academics, artists and writers, including, most recently, Pandelis Prevelakis whose *Tale of a Town* is a powerful personal history of Rethymnon. The liveliest area is around Petichaki Square, although the beach is also lined with restaurants and cafés. There is a wine festival in the public gardens every July (see **Events**) and in Nov. there are festivities commemorating the 1866 explosion at Moni Arkadi (see **Events**, **A-Z**). See RETHYMNON.

Rethymnon

Rimondi Fountain, Rethymnon: This early-17thC fountain, facing the bustling cafés around Petichaki Square, was named after the Venetian rector Alvise Arimondi. It is decorated with columns and lions' heads, and once served as an important source of drinking water for the town's inhabitants. See **RETHYMNON-ATTRACTIONS**.

St. Titus: The patron saint of Crete and the first bishop of Gortys (see **A-Z**). St. Titus was an early Christian missionary to the island, directed there by St. Paul in his New Testament *Epistle to Titus*. The basilica of Agios Titus in Gortys (see **HERAKLION-EXCURSION 1**) and the church of the same name at Heraklion (see **HERAKLION-ATTRACTIONS**) are named in memory of the saint. St. Titus' Day is 25 Aug. and is celebrated with processions in Heraklion.

Samaria Gorge: A walk through the famous gorge is one of the best-known excursions on Crete. The 18 km trek from the Omalos Plateau down to the south coast, or vice versa, is an extremely strenuous one, and can be tricky in places. Every year there are incidents (broken legs, heart attacks, and injuries from falling rocks). You must, therefore, be reasonably fit and only attempt the walk with proper clothing, stout footwear and protection from the sun. It is safest and most convenient to go with an organized tour as the guides carry radios with which to call for assistance. Many travel agencies sell tickets for the bus trip and walk (4000-6000 Drs). The gorge can only be entered between the months of May and Oct. since the water level rises, making it impassable in winter.

Samaria Gorge

Sendoni Cave: 45 km southeast of Rethymnon on the outskirts of the village of Zoniana. The dimensions of this cave, which has only recently been opened to the public, are impressive – 500 m long and an area of 3300 sq. m. During the low season the key can be obtained from the keeper in the village (next to the church). See **Caves**.

Sfakia: A region on the slopes of the White Mountains which is renowned for defending Cretan liberty against foreign invasion and occupation. The capital, Chora Sfakion, was a flourishing commercial port up to the 18thC. Due to its geographical position, Sfakia remained quite independent from the rest of the island, and there are various monuments in the area which bear witness to its bloody and heroic past. The area is now fairly busy because of the popularity of excursions to the Samaria Gorge (see **A-Z**). Nevertheless, Sfakia manages to retain an air of detachment from the rest of the island.

Sitia: See **AGIOS NIKOLAOS-BEACHES, EXCURSION 1**.

Spili: See **RETHYMNON-EXCURSION**.

Spinalonga: A small island in the gulf of Mirabello which was, until 1957, a leper colony housing up to 400 patients. In earlier times the strategically important island was the site of a Venetian fortress designed to defend the coast against Turkish forces. Built in 1579, it managed to withstand various assaults before it was surrendered in 1715. You can still see its ruins. See AGIOS NIKOLAOS-ATTRACTIONS.

Vathipetro: 15 km south of Heraklion. The recently discovered site of a large Minoan villa set in the middle of a fertile agricultural area. The original multistorey building contained large rooms and basement workshops. Many interesting objects have been found here relating to the everyday life of the time, including wine and oil presses, weaving tools and what was probably a kiln. 0800-1530 Mon.-Fri.

Venizelos, Eleftherias (1864-1936): One of Greece's leading political figures. Born in Mournies (near Chania) in 1864, he attempted to lead a revolution in 1905. The revolt failed but Venizelos eventually became prime minister of Greece in 1910. He was the architect of the Union of Crete with Greece in 1913 and is a greatly revered historical figure on the island where there are various memorials to him (you can see his statue in Platia Eleftherias – Liberty Square – in Heraklion). There are also exhibits relating to him in Chania's Historical Museum & Archives (see CHANIA-ATTRACTIONS) and Venizelos House. He died in exile in Paris in 1936, having survived two assassination attempts, and is buried in Akrotiri.

Zakros: 45 km southeast of Sitia. Nikolaos Platon identified this site at the eastern end of Crete as the fourth-largest centre of the Minoan civilization after earlier excavations (at the beginning of the century) of the ancient town had been abandoned. Full-scale excavation began again in 1962 and the palace was found very quickly. It was largely destroyed in 1450 BC when its inhabitants fled with their belongings. Nevertheless, the site has yielded a great many interesting archaeological finds and treasures, some of which can be seen in Sitia Museum and others in the Archaeological Museum at Heraklion (see HERAKLION-ATTRACTIONS, A-Z). See AGIOS NIKOLAOS-ATTRACTIONS, EXCURSION 1.

Accidents & Breakdowns: In the event of an accident, exchange names and insurance details. Only expect police intervention if someone has been injured, in which case you should contact your consulate (see **A-Z**). If you break down, call the ELPA (Hellenic Touring & Automobile Club) which offers a free breakdown service to members of foreign automobile associations, tel: 157. If you are not eligible for this service, contact Express Service, tel: 154. See **Driving**, **Emergency Numbers**.

Accommodation: There are six official categories of hotel on Crete, ranging from Luxury through grades A to E (the last being pretty basic). The quality of the accommodation varies tremendously within each category but the price is fixed by the government. A double room costs 15,000 Drs per night in a Luxury hotel and 2500 Drs in an E-class hotel. The larger hotels are usually booked up with group reservations, so don't automatically expect to find a room in one of them. If you arrive in Crete without a hotel reservation, go to the NTOG office at Chania or Heraklion airports (see **Tourist Information**), or to a travel agent or the tourist police (see **Police**). There are also many rooms to rent in private houses, especially in villages, which are simple but good value. Self-catering villas and apartments can be very reasonable too but usually need to be booked in advance. See **Camping**, **Youth Hostels**.

Airports: There are two main airports on Crete:
Heraklion, tel: 081-228426, 3 km east of the capital. Handles international flights, daily flights to Rhodes, Mykonos and Athens (seven), and air links to other islands. Airport facilities include an information desk, duty-free shop, restaurant, meeting point and car hire representatives. Olympic Airways runs a bus link to Heraklion (300 Drs) and there is

also a cheaper local bus service (150 Drs). The same journey by taxi costs c. 1000 Drs.

Chania, tel: 0821-63245, 15 km from Chania town. Mainly handles internal and charter flights. The airport is smaller than Heraklion's and there are fewer facilities. The Olympic Airways bus link to town costs 300 Drs, the local bus costs 150 Drs and taxis cost c. 2000 Drs.

In addition, a very small airport at Sitia, tel: 0843-24666, operates flights to Rhodes, via the islands of Kassos and Karpathos, four times a week. The Olympic Airways office in Sitia is situated at Venizelou Street 56, tel: 0843-22270/22596.

Antiques: It is illegal to take Greek antiques out of the country without prior permission, which involves an enormous amount of paperwork, and those found guilty of illegally exporting antiques face prosecution and stiff penalties. It is probably advisable to settle for some of the excellent copies of ancient icons and antique jewellery available on the island, or else try to find old embroidery and costumes in the various flea markets.

Baby-sitters: Ask at your hotel reception or speak to your travel representative. The service is likely to cost about 1000 Drs per hr. See **Children**.

Banks: See **Currency**, **Money**, **Opening Times**.

Beaches: There are marvellous beaches with clear water to be found all round the coastline of Crete but the best and generally the quieter beaches are in the south. Some beaches do suffer from oil pollution and the water is not always clean, especially near the larger towns. Some of the bigger hotels have private beaches and there are also municipal beaches, popular with families, which have showers and changing cabins (and cost upwards of 350 Drs). You can hire canoes, pedal boats and windsurfing boards, or water-ski, at most of the resort beaches. Always be careful of strong currents and undertow. See the **BEACHES** topic pages for **AGIOS NIKOLAOS**, **CHANIA**, **HERAKLION** and **RETHYMNON**, **Sport**.

Best Buys: As on most of the Greek islands, local crafts are the best buys. These include jewellery, leather goods, pottery, knitwear and embroidery. All are widely available in the numerous arts and crafts shops in the tourist centres but try shopping around for quality. For example, in the villages you can try bargaining directly with the craftspeople but don't underestimate the skills and materials involved. Leather work is particularly abundant in the west of Crete, where it is possible to have shoes made to measure, while the whole of the northern coast, and especially Heraklion, is renowned for its pottery which can be purchased direct from the workshops. The island is also well known for its cloth. *Hyfanda* is the type of weaving (see **Crafts**) that is particular to Crete and many designs are available in it – the centres at Kritsa (see **AGIOS NIKOLAOS-ATTRACTIONS**, **A-Z**) and Anogia (see **HERAKLION-EXCURSION 2**) both produce high-quality work. Woollens are another good buy and hand-knitted pullovers are extremely good value. Speciality foods include olive oil, *feta* (goats' milk cheese), herbs, nougat, dried fruit and honey, which can all be found in the local markets (see **A-Z**).

Bicycle & Motorcycle Hire: Available in the larger towns and villages frequented by tourists. Bicycles are ideal for exploring the immediate vicinity and finding quieter beaches, although the ruggedness of the terrain combined with the summer heat may make the going a bit difficult. Motorcycles are good for longer distances and avoiding the traffic jams in Heraklion and Chania, but strong winds on the northern coast and rocky dirt roads can be hazardous, so take extra care. You will probably find that scooters lack sufficient power to propel two people up some of the steep roads in the interior. Helmets are seldom provided but try and acquire one for your own safety.
Bicycles – c. 1000 Drs per day.
Scooters – c. 4000 Drs per day.
Motorcycles – 5000-7000 Drs per day (when you hire by the week you get two days free).
The minimum age for hiring scooters and motorcycles is 18. A licence is required for larger models of motorcycle. Make sure that comprehensive insurance is included in the agreement as, unfortunately, there are many accidents each year caused by inexperienced or careless drivers.

Budget: 1992 prices. Crete is still relatively inexpensive, although prices continue to rise in proportion to the growing number of tourists coming to the island.

Bread (small loaf)	150 Drs
Butter (200 g)	420 Drs
Eggs (half a dozen)	200 Drs
Fruit juice (1 litre)	250 Drs
Wine (70 cl)	650 Drs
Hotel breakfast	c. 500 Drs
Lunch	c. 1000 Drs
Dinner (inc. wine)	from 2000 Drs

Buses: Crete has two types of bus service: local buses, used by the islanders for getting to schools and markets; and KTEL for longer journeys, which are usually more modern. Tourist attractions usually have regular services but buses serving the smaller villages may run at inconvenient times for day excursions.

Heraklion bus stations: Terminus A at the port serves the east coast of the island; Terminus B at Porta Chania serves the southwest along inland roads; the station near the Venetian harbour serves the west coast; the smallest station at Kiprou Square, just outside the walls, serves the southeast (mainly Ierapetra).
Chania bus stations: Buses to Rethymnon/Heraklion from Eleftherias Venizelou Square 28; buses to Kissamos/Selina from Kebaidi Square; buses to Apokoronos/Sfakia from Nikiforou/Episkopou.
Rethymnon bus station: Buses to Chania/Heraklion from Agnostou Stratioti Square.
Agios Nikolaos bus stations: Atlandithos Square for services to Heraklion, Sitia, Ierapetra and villages along the way; the harbour for buses to Elounda.
Sitia bus station: Papanastasiou Street 4.
The termini in the provincial capitals have cafés and toilets (see **A-Z**).

Cameras & Photography: Films, video cassettes and flashbulbs are all readily available in the provincial capitals and tourist centres but they are expensive so stock up before leaving the UK. You can sometimes take photographs in museums and at archaeological sites. There are restrictions on taking photographs near military or naval installations (such as the naval base at Soudha bay). You can hire video equipment in the larger resorts.

Camping: There are 14 official camp sites on Crete, the most popular being those at Paleochora, Agia Galini, Matala, Chersonisos, Heraklion, Malia and Ierapetra. These provide all the usual facilities and are generally fairly clean and well run. Contact any of the NTOG offices (see **Tourist Information**) for a list of local camp sites. The average costs per night are 600 Drs for an adult and 300 Drs for a child, with a tent; cars are extra. Unofficial camping is now theoretically prohibited on the island, though it is still practised, especially in more remote areas.

Car Hire: This can be fairly expensive but is one of the best ways to see the island. In theory you are required to hold an international driving licence but in practice most agencies will accept a national one that has been valid for at least a year. The minimum age for hiring a car varies from 21 to 25. Local agencies tend to be cheaper than the well-known international firms but check that they offer comprehensive insurance. The larger firms have the advantage in that they cover the whole island, allowing you to pick up and drop off a car at different places. They will also provide a replacement in the case of theft or breakdown. However, you will have to leave an extremely large deposit unless you pay by credit card. Try negotiating for a lower rate out of season. See **Driving**.

Chemists: The sign for a chemist is a green or red cross on a white background. Most chemists keep normal opening times but they also operate a rota system so that at least one shop is open outside these hours. Details are displayed in the window of every chemist. See **Health**.

Children: The Cretan people adore children and make them welcome in most establishments, even late at night. Most public gardens in the provincial capitals provide swings and slides, and there is often a funfair just outside the one in Heraklion. Most of the larger hotels also provide amenities to keep children amused. If your child gets lost contact the tourist police (see **Police**). See **Baby-sitters**.

Climate: Spring (average temperature 15°C-21°C) and autumn (18°C-21°C) are probably the best times to visit Crete, as the weather is not too hot and the sea is warm enough to swim in. The island is at its greenest and most colourful in spring. The hottest months are July and Aug. (25°C-30°C) but the summer temperatures are mitigated by the prevailing meltemi, a seasonal wind blowing from the north. Winters are mild and often quite wet.

Complaints: Crete relies heavily on tourism, so you are unlikely to be overcharged. However, if you do feel that you have been unfairly treated, ask to see the owner or manager of the premises. If you are still not satisfied, then you can report the establishment to the tourist police (see **Police**), but you will find that just threatening this course of action is usually sufficient.

Consulates:
UK – Papalexandrou Road 16, Heraklion, Crete, tel: 081-224012/234127.
Republic of Ireland – Vass. Constantinou 7, Athens, tel: 723-2771/2405.
USA – Vas. Sofias Avenue 91, Athens, tel: 721-2951.
Canada – Gennadiou 4, Athens, tel: 723-9511.
Australia – Dimitriou Soutso 37, Athens, tel: 644-7303.
New Zealand – An Tsocha Street 15-17, Athens, tel: 641-0314.

Conversion Chart:

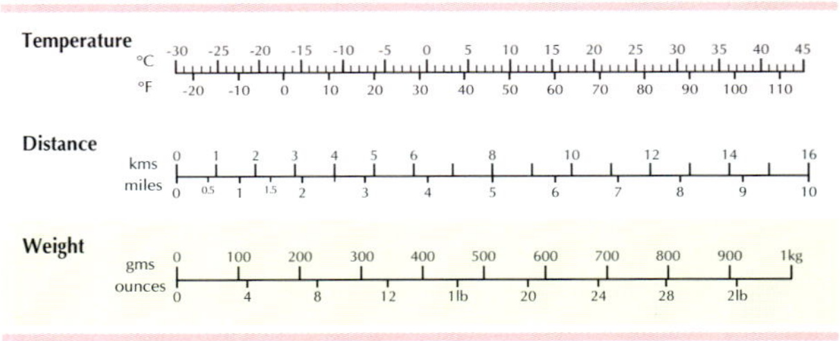

Crime & Theft: The Cretan people are renowned for being honest and trustworthy, and theft on Crete is rare (another tourist is more likely to rob you than a Cretan). Nevertheless, take care of your property and leave valuables in the hotel safe. If you are the victim of a theft, contact the police (see **A-Z**). Remember to keep a copy of the police report for any insurance claim you may make (see **Insurance**). If you are arrested for any reason, your consulate (see **A-Z**) is obliged to find you an English-speaking lawyer. See **Emergency Numbers**.

Currency: The drachma is Greece's monetary unit (abbreviated as Drs). Coins in circulation are worth 5, 10, 20, 50 and 100 Drs. Notes are in denominations of 50, 100, 500, 1000 and 5000 Drs. See **Money**.

Customs: The *volta*, an early-evening, pre-dinner promenade, is very much a social institution. In the capital, head for Eleftherias Square if you want to join the crowd. Don't be offended by the Greeks' curiosity which should be taken as a sign of genuine interest. In Cretan homes it is customary for the mistress of the house to ply a visitor with food and refreshments without taking any herself – accept any hospitality proffered to you gracefully. Never make a gesture with the palm of your hand facing outwards as this is considered grossly insulting. Lastly, if you are told that something will be ready tomorrow (*avrio*), it may not necessarily mean the next day. See **Ceremonies**, **Language**.

Customs Allowances:

UK/EC	Cigarettes	Cigarillos	Cigars	Tobacco	Still Table Wine	Spirits/Liqueurs	Fortified Wine	Additional Still Table Wine	Perfume	Toilet Water	Gifts & Souvenirs
Duty Free	**200** *or*	**100** *or*	**50** *or*	**250 g**	**2 *l***	**1 *l*** *or*	**2 *l*** *or*	**2 *l***	**60 cc/ml**	**250 cc/ml**	**£32**
Duty Paid	**800**	**400**	**200**	**1 kg**	**90 *l*****	**10 *l***	**20 *l***				

* Of which no more than 60 l should be sparkling wine.

Since 1 Jan. 1993 restrictions on allowances for duty-paid goods brought into the UK from any EC country have been abolished. Travellers are now able to buy goods, including alcoholic drinks and tobacco, paying duty and VAT in the EC country where the goods are purchased. However, duty-paid goods should be for the traveller's own use and carried by him personally. Whereas previously there were either-or options, travellers can now bring back the sum of the goods in the duty-paid column.

Disabled People: Crete has few facilities for disabled people. In addition, the general lack of organization and the mountainous nature of the landscape can make things very difficult for the handicapped. It may not be possible to obtain certain medicines, so be sure to stock up at home before you go on holiday. See **Health**, **Insurance**.

Drinks: Crete boasts a variety of different wines, ranging from the well-known Vin Castel to the red, robust wines of the Sitia region and the excellent wines of Archanes and Peza. The ones you are most likely to encounter on Cretan supermarket shelves are Minos, Demestica, Gortys, Olympia and Lato. Of course, the distinctive retsina, a resinated

wine which is best drunk cold and is a good accompaniment to many meals (something of an acquired taste), is available all over Greece. Ouzo, the other national drink, is the most common apéritif. This aniseed spirit is served with water and ice. Metaxa is a Greek brandy that is sweeter and often rougher than its French counterpart, although it comes in a range (one to seven stars) of qualities. Beer is extremely popular on the island. Both of the local brands, Fix and Hellas, are widely available, as are imported lagers. Raki (*tzikoudia*), an exceptionally strong spirit, is something of a Cretan speciality. Served in little glasses, usually as a *digestif*, it should be swallowed in one gulp! Greek coffee comes in very small cups, is extremely strong and black, and is served with a glass of water. Order it *glikos* if you want it very sweet, *metrios* for medium sweet and *sketos* for plain. If you don't want it at all ask for a Nescafé. You can drink the tap water but most people prefer to buy bottled water which is available nearly everywhere.

Driving: You must have an EC or international driving licence and third-party insurance to drive in Greece. Green Card insurance is also recommended. Drive on the right-hand side and give way to traffic coming from the right. Seat belts are now compulsory. The one main road running along the north coast of the island from Chania to Sitia is in good condition and there is a provincial network of secondary roads which are nearly all surfaced but are less well maintained and are pitted by occasional potholes. The mountain roads are narrow with incredibly sharp bends. Be sure to sound your horn as you approach bends as Cretan driving tends to be fast and erratic and many people, and stray animals, walk on the roads. Don't embark on any journeys by car without a detailed map as many roads are not well signposted and you could easily lose your way. In Heraklion, cars with even registration numbers can only be used on even-numbered dates and cars with odd numbers can only be used on odd dates but this does not apply to foreign or rented cars. Observe the local speed limits and parking regulations, and don't drink and drive as this is an offence. See **Accidents & Breakdowns**, **Car Hire**, **Parking**, **Petrol**.

Drugs: All drugs are illegal and there are severe penalties for offenders, ranging from prison sentences of up to one year for possession of even small amounts of hashish, to life imprisonment and hefty fines for anyone suspected of dealing in drugs.

Eating Out: There are restaurants catering for every taste in all the larger towns and tourist resorts, but the smaller villages generally only possess tavernas, which are usually more informal, cheaper, family-run establishments where you will often be invited into the kitchen to choose what you want to eat. For authentic Greek cooking go to a taverna frequented by local people, even if the décor is not inspiring (spontaneous dancing may start later on in the evening). Desserts are not usually served in tavernas (although this is changing to cater for foreign tastes) and it is customary to go to a pastry shop after a meal. Before the meal it is traditional to go for an appetizer at an *ouzeri* where you will be served with ouzo and snacks known as mezedes. There is a tradition of serving food lukewarm, and sometimes several courses appear at once. Specify if you want things done differently. The menu in restaurants and tavernas, when there is one, always has two sets of prices (with and without service charges). You pay the more expensive of the two. See the **RESTAURANTS** topic pages for **AGIOS NIKOLAOS**, **CHANIA**, **HERAKLION** and **RETHYMNON**, **Food**.

ΑΡΟΣ
ΑΡΟΤΑΒΕΡΝΑ
FRISCHER FISCH
FRESH FISH
FISHSOUP
trivsel
boutari

Electricity: 220 V. Small two-pin plugs are used and adaptors are available in Greece and the UK.

Emergency Numbers:

Police	100
Ambulance	166
Fire	199
Tourist police	171

Events:

6 January (Epiphany): Blessing of the Water, a ceremony (intended to chase away the spirits of the twelve days of Christmas) in which a cross is blessed then thrown into the water. Young men and boys dive in to retrieve it and the winner receives a cash prize.
Fortnight before Lent: Carnival, costumed processions and festivities best enjoyed in Heraklion and Rethymnon; *Last Mon. before Lent:* Clean Monday, a day to fly kites and take picnics before the period of abstinence begins.
Easter weekend (Greek Orthodox calendar): Ceremonies, processions, church services, the lighting of candles, fireworks, celebrations and feasting.
25 March: Independence Day, processions and general celebrations to commemorate the revolt against the Turks in 1821.
1 May: May Day or Spring Festival, a national holiday with dancing and feasting; *20-27:* Anniversary of the Battle of Crete (World War II), dancing, sports events and ceremonies in Chania and a different village each year.
24 June: Feast of St. John the Baptist and Summer Solstice, bonfires all over the island; *Late June:* Naval or Marine Week, fireworks, naval displays and sea sports, especially at Soudha.
15-31 July: Rethymnon Wine Festival, folk dancing and the sampling of wines.
July-August: Heraklion Festival, cultural events include drama, dance, classical music, jazz and films.
15 August: Assumption of the Virgin Mary, dancing, fireworks, sports and craft displays, pilgrimage to the island of Tinos, feasts in many

villages and at many monasteries, but chiefly celebrated in Mokhos (near Malia) and Neapoli; *31:* Consecration of the Virgin, festivals and dancing at Psychro village on the Lasithi plateau.
28 October: Ochi ('No') Day, national holiday commemorating Greece's rejection of Mussolini's ultimatum of 1940.
7-9 November: Moni Arkadi Explosion, large celebration commemorating those who died in the 1886 explosion at Moni Arkadi (see **A-Z**).
See **Festivities**, **Public Holidays**.

Ferries: Chania and Heraklion are the main departure points for Piraeus (the port of Athens), the Peloponnese, the Dodecanese and the Cyclades, though there are also sailings from Agios Nikolaos, Kastelli and Sitia.
Chania's port is at Soudha, 7 km west of the town. Local buses leave from the marketplace (see **CHANIA-ATTRACTIONS**) every 15 min (approx.). Most of the ferries for Piraeus arrive in the morning and leave in the evening: Tue., Thu. & Sat. in winter, daily in summer. The journey takes 11 hr and tickets cost 4000 Drs per person and at least 6000 Drs for a car. There are agents on Halidon Street and at the port.
Heraklion's port has two ferry services per day to Piraeus, taking 12 hr; tickets cost 4000 Drs per person. There are also ferries to many other destinations, including Mykonos (via Santorini, Ios, Naxos and Paros), Cyprus and Egypt. Port facilities include a bar, restaurant, post office, telephones, toilets, showers and an information service.
Rethymnon has a picturesque little port with four overnight services per week to Piraeus. The agent for Rethymniaki is at Arkadhou 250, tel: 29221/21518.
Agios Nikolaos is served by two lines running to the Dodecanese and the Cyclades. Services run Wed. & Sat. in summer but infrequently in winter. The agent is Massaros Travel, Koundourou, tel: 22267.

Food: Typical Greek dishes include:
Moussaka – Aubergines, minced meat, potatoes and béchamel sauce.
Pastitsio – Macaroni, minced meat and béchamel sauce.
Dolmades – Stuffed vine leaves.
Souvlaki – Pieces of meat cooked on a skewer, served with spices and

tomatoes, or in pitta bread with salad. The Greek equivalent of a kebab.

Keftedhes – Spicy meatballs.

Taramasalata – Salad dip of fish roe mixed with cream, olive oil and garlic.

Tzatziki – Cucumber, yoghurt and garlic salad dip.

Greek salad – *Feta* (goats' milk cheese), tomatoes, cucumbers, peppers and olives.

Mezedes – A variety of small dishes served with an apéritif (traditionally an ouzo – see **Drinks**) or as a starter.

Hummus – Puréed chickpeas, tahini (sesame paste), lemon juice, garlic and olive oil served as a starter.

Local specialities:

Mizithra – Unsalted cream cheese used in pies (*bougatsa*).

Yaourti – Yoghurt often served with honey for breakfast.

Madares – Meat stew with cheese and potatoes.

Kallitsounia – Cheese and cinnamon pie.

Barbounia – Red mullet served whole (expensive and bony).

Calamari – Rings of squid fried in batter.

See the **RESTAURANTS** topic pages for **AGIOS NIKOLAOS**, **CHANIA**, **HERAKLION** and **RETHYMNON**, **Eating Out**.

Guides: There is no official list of approved guides. If you want an individual tour try one of the many tour operators (see below) in the main resorts who will arrange it for you. If you can find a taxi driver who speaks good English and knows the sights, this would be another option but always arrange a price beforehand. There are always guides at the main attractions who will approach you at the ticket desk, where

their cost should be displayed. Below are some reputable firms who organize fully guided excursions to the main sights such as Knossos, Samaria, Spinalonga and the Lasithi Plateau:
Panos Travel, S. Venizelou Street 19, Agios Nikolaos, tel: 0841-26149.
Kera Tours, Sof. Venizelou Street 21, Agios Nikolaos, tel: 0841-26496.
Golden Island Tours, Halidon Street 87, Chania, tel: 0821-41458.
Neorio Travel, I. Kondilaki 55, Rethymnon, tel: 0831-23169.
IDA Travel, Chortazi Street, Rethymnon, tel: 0831-24466.

Health: Before leaving the UK you should obtain form E111 from the Department of Social Security which entitles you to free medical treatment in Greece (present it to any State doctor you consult, who will arrange for you to be exempted from payment). However, standards of health care in Greece are less than adequate and it is also advisable to take out a private health insurance policy to cover private treatment and the cost of repatriation in case of serious illness (see **Insurance**).
The following are hospitals with outpatient departments:
General State Hospital, Dragoumi Street, Chania, tel: 0821-27231.
Rethymnon Hospital, Hiliakaki Street, Rethymnon, tel: 0831-29271.
Venizelou Hospital (near Knossos), Heraklion, tel: 081-239502.
For treatment in Agios Nikolaos, tel: 0841-22369; and in Sitia, tel: 0843-22231.
If you have any trouble finding an English-speaking doctor, contact the NTOG office (see **Tourist Information**). There are no vaccination requirements unless you are coming from a country where there has been an epidemic. See **Chemists**, **Disabled People**.

Insurance: You should take out travel insurance covering you against theft and loss of property and money, as well as medical expenses, for the duration of your stay. Your travel agent should be able to recommend a suitable policy. See **Crime & Theft**, **Driving**, **Health**.

Language: Many casual visitors to Greece are put off any attempt to master the Greek language by the unfamiliar alphabet and the importance of pronouncing words with the proper stress. More problems arise from the transliteration of Greek words into English (especially in place names), as it is possible to be confronted with several variations. For example, Heraklion can also be spelt as Iraklion and Herakleion; Chania may appear as Khania or Hania; and Agios Nikolaos might be written as Ayios Nikolaos. However, it is worthwhile trying to learn a few basic phrases as this will be appreciated by the local inhabitants. *Collins Greek Phrase Book & Dictionary* is recommended. See **Customs**.

Laundries: Launderettes are rare on Crete and any available laundry services tend to be expensive. Some of the hotels may offer the service to their guests. Otherwise you may as well do your own washing – it will dry very quickly in the warm climate.

Lost Property: If you lose anything, contact the local tourist police (see **Police**) and the chances are you will recover it.

Markets: Crete has many lively, colourful markets where you can find a variety of local products ranging from food and crafts to cheap household goods and clothes. The food market in Chania is a dominant feature of the town (see **CHANIA-ATTRACTIONS**). Here you can buy the

0
1
2
3
4
5

medicinal plant called *dictamo*, which is used to make a herbal tea and is also rumoured to be an aphrodisiac. Rethymnon has a picturesque market in the centre of town which offers both foodstuffs and crafts for sale. The market in 1866 Street in Heraklion (near Venizelou Square) sells oil, honey, plants, wine, fruit and cheeses, as well as crafts and antiques. See **Best Buys**.

Money: The main branches of the top banks represented on Crete, the National Bank of Greece, the Ionian Bank and the Commercial Bank, are to be found along 25 Avgoustou Street in Heraklion, with smaller branches in the provincial capitals, the larger villages and tourist resorts. Traveller's cheques and Eurocheques can be cashed in banks, bureaux de change and at post offices (see **A-Z**). Some of the larger shops will accept them as well as the more common currencies, such as pounds sterling, dollars, francs and Deutschmarks, but offer a lower rate of exchange. Check what this is before you enter into a transaction. Hotels also provide round-the-clock exchange facilities but again check the rate and their charges before you change money or cash traveller's cheques. Credit cards and traveller's cheques are accepted by many of the larger, more expensive restaurants, shops, hotels and car-hire firms. Remember to take your passport when changing money and cheques. See **Currency**, **Opening Times**.

Newspapers: Foreign newspapers, both tabloids and quality, are widely available at kiosks the day after publication. The English-language *Athens News* is also found everywhere there is a market for it, and covers both Greek and international news. See **What's On**.

Nightlife: Cretans tend to eat late and often stay up until the early hours drinking and dancing. Most discos and bars are intended to cater for tourists so if you want a more authentic evening try a bouzouki bar. The NTOG (see **Tourist Information**) can provide up-to-date information on current dance and theatre performances, although the best examples of traditional folk dancing (see **A-Z**) are probably to be seen at the local saints' day celebrations known as *panegyria* (see **Festivities**). There are also cinemas in Crete which are usually open air

and show foreign films subtitled into Greek. See the **NIGHTLIFE** topic pages for **AGIOS NIKOLAOS**, **CHANIA**, **HERAKLION** and **RETHYMNON**.

Nudism: Topless sunbathing is tolerated in Greece away from town beaches but nudism is officially prohibited and can greatly offend local people. Despite this it can be practised with discretion on some of the more remote stretches of sand and in more isolated coves.

Opening Times: These vary considerably from place to place and season to season, are subject to frequent changes and can also depend on the vagaries of the owner or manager. This is especially true of the discos and nightclubs which exist purely to cater for the tourists and will open earlier if there is a demand for them, or close when there are too few customers to make it worthwhile staying open. The following times, therefore, are very general:
NTOG offices (see **Tourist Information**) – 0800-1400, 1700-2000 Mon.-Fri., 0800-1400 Sat. & Sun., but 0800-2200 daily in summer.
Post offices – 0800-1900 Mon.-Fri. in some resorts, 0800-1400 Mon.-Fri. in others.

Banks – 0800-1400 Mon.-Thu., 0800-1330 Fri. In addition, during the summer at least one bank in each of the provincial capitals re-opens 1700-1900 for changing money and on Sat. for the same purpose.
Restaurants – 1200-1500, 1830-late (most stop serving at 2400).
Shops – 0800-1430 Mon., Wed. & Sat., 0800-1400, 1730-2000 Tue., Thu. & Fri. Many shops in busy resorts now stay open in the afternoon to cater for tourists.
OTE offices (see **Telephones & Telegrams**) – Open 24 hr in Heraklion and Chania but in smaller towns they close at 2200.

Orientation: Crete, the largest and most southerly of the Greek islands, is divided up into four nomes or provinces – Heraklion, Chania, Lasithi and Rethymnon – the capitals of which are Heraklion, Chania, Agios Nikolaos and Rethymnon. This geographical distinction has been followed in the topic section of this guide. It is strongly suggested that you purchase as detailed a road map of Crete as you can before visiting the island. NTOG offices (see **Tourist Information**) in the provincial capitals or at the airports and car-hire firms can provide town plans pinpointing the chief sights, hotels, etc. In Greek addresses the street number follows the street name but outside the city centre the number that appears in this position may represent a block rather than individual premises (the number of which may appear afterwards in brackets). In giving addresses this guidebook uses the English for 'Street', 'Avenue' and 'Square', which in Greek are Odhos, Leoforos and Platia respectively.

Parking: Parking is really only a problem in the narrow streets of the main town centres which you would be well advised to avoid anyway. Where parking is prohibited, the kerbstones are often painted orange. Where parking is restricted or where you have to pay to park there are usually signs, often in English. For example, along the waterfront at Rethymnon you are asked to buy a ticket for 1 or 2 hr at the town hall or from kiosks. See **Driving**.

Passports & Customs: A valid passport (or identity card for EC visitors) is necessary but no visa is required for stays of less than three months for British, EC, Australian, New Zealand and Canadian nationals.

For longer stays, apply for an extension from the local police (see **A-Z**) – you may be asked to show proof of financial resources. US visitors can stay for two months without a visa. See **Customs Allowances**.

Petrol: There are plenty of petrol stations around the island but they are few and far between in the more remote regions of the south, so fill your tank before attempting any excursions into the hinterland. Four-star (200 Drs per litre), unleaded (185 Drs per litre) and diesel (130 Drs per litre) are available everywhere. Opening hours are variable and unreliable. You will be served, and credit cards (Visa and Access) are accepted at the larger stations on the north coast. See **Driving**.

Police: Apart from the regular police, who wear green uniforms and deal with crime, traffic offences, etc., there are also the tourist police, tel: 104, who wear a dark grey-blue uniform and badges (national flags) indicating which foreign languages they speak. Their role is to help tourists in trouble and investigate any complaints about hotels, restaurant prices, etc.
Main police stations:
Karaiskaki Street, Chania, tel: 0821-24477; Arkdhion, Rethymnon, tel: 0831-22231; Dikeossinis Street, Heraklion, tel: 081-283190/282031; Omirou Street 7, Agios Nikolaos, tel: 0841-22321/22251; and if you are in Sitia, tel: 0843-24200/22266.
See **Crime & Theft**, **Emergency Numbers**.

Post Offices: All registered letters and parcels should be handed over to the clerk unsealed as the contents will have to be checked. It is cheaper to buy stamps in post offices than at kiosks where they are 10% more expensive. Postboxes are yellow. Poste restante services are fairly reliable but be sure to mark the name of the post office clearly.
Main post offices:
Gianiri Street (near Eleftherias Square), Heraklion; Tzanakaki Street 3-5, Chania; P. Koundouriotou Street 92, Rethymnon; 28 Octovriou Street, Agios Nikolaos; Kothri Square, Ierapetra; and Evrikes Antistasis Street 2, Sitia.
See **Opening Times**.

Public Holidays: 1 Jan. (New Year's Day), 6 Jan. (Epiphany), 25 Mar. (Independence Day), First day of Lent (Clean Monday), Good Fri. (movable feast), Easter Mon. (movable feast), Ascension Day (movable feast), 1 May (Labour Day), Whit Mon. (movable feast), 15 Aug. (Assumption), 28 Oct. (Ochi Day), 25 Dec. (Christmas Day), 26 Dec. (St. Stephen's Day).

Rabies: There are no recorded cases of rabies on the island.

Religious Services: The only other services apart from those of the Greek Orthodox Church are Roman Catholic Masses held at the Catholic churches in Heraklion, Chania, Rethymnon and Agios Nikolaos every Sat. and Sun.

Shopping: See **Best Buys**, **Markets**.

Smoking: There do not seem to be any restrictions on smoking except at petrol stations. People smoke freely in restaurants and on public transport.

Sport:
Fishing – Rod fishing is permitted everywhere but harpooning is limited to Falasarna, Sfinari, Sougia and Sfakia in the Chania region; Panormos and Agia Galini in the Rethymnon region; Agia Pelagia, Chersonisos, Malia, Lendas, Kaloi Limenes and Tsoutsouros in the Heraklion region; and Agios Nikolaos, Mohlos, Palekastro, Myrtos and around Spinalonga and Chryssi in the Lasithi region.
Tennis – Chania Tennis Club, Dimokratias Street, tel: 0821-24010/ 21293; Heraklion Tennis Club, Dukos Beufaurt Street, tel: 081-226152 (after 1400). Both clubs have five courts and it is also possible to arrange lessons.
Horse riding – Karteros Riding Club, Amnisos, tel: 081-282005 (lessons and trekking).
Diving – Elounda Beach Hotel, Elounda, tel: 0841-41412; Peninsula Hotel, Agia Pelagia, tel: 081-289404.
Windsurfing – Boards for hire at Neas Choras, Maleme, Halyves,

Kournas Lake, Almyrida, Kastelli, Rethymnon, Agia Galini, Adele, Bali and Plakias, Chersonisos harbour, Malia, Agia Pelagia, Agios Nikolaos, Kalo Chorio, Elounda, Ierapetra and Sitia.
Water-skiing – Instruction available at Chania Marine Club, Akti Kanari, tel: 0821-24387; Chersonisos harbour; Malia; and Agia Pelagia.
Mountaineering & skiing – The Greek Alpine Club (EOS) has refuges at Volikas and Kallergi in the White Mountains, and on Mount Ida. For information and keys contact the EOS offices at Stratigou Tzanaki Street 90, Chania, tel: 0821-24647; Dikeosinis Street 53, Heraklion, tel: 081-287110; or Arkadias Street 143, Rethymnon, tel: 0831-22411.

Taxis: Taxis are moderately priced and plentiful. Most villages have at least one taxi and there are lots in the resorts and provincial towns. Although most drivers are honest and friendly, make sure that the meter is running, and for longer journeys agree a price beforehand. There are the usual surcharges for items of luggage, journeys late at night, etc., plus a fee for waiting time. It may be worthwhile hiring a taxi for a day excursion when the bus times prove inconvenient, especially if there are enough of you to share the cost. See **Tipping**.

Telephones & Telegrams: Metered international telephone calls can be made from OTE (Greek Telecommunications Organization) offices or from telephone boxes distinguished by an orange band, which take 20 and 50 Drs coins.
Main OTE offices:
Tzanakaki Street 3-5, Chania; Koundourioti Street, Rethymnon; Minotavrou Street (behind Venizelos Square), Heraklion; 25 Martiou Street, Agios Nikolaos; Koraka Street, Ierapetra; and Sifis Street, Sitia.
You may find that you have to queue for rather a long time, and the waiting time for connections can also be considerable.
To direct dial abroad dial 00 followed by the code for the country (UK – 44, USA – 1, Ireland – 353), then remember to omit the first zero of the city code.

International operator	161
Local operator	151
Directory enquiries	131

Telegrams (in Greece)	155
International telegrams	165
Telexes	181

It is cheaper to phone abroad 2100-0900 and at weekends.
Telegrams can be sent from OTE offices or by telephone (see above). See **Emergency Numbers**, **Opening Times**.

Television & Radio: There are daily English-language news broadcasts and tourist information items on local radio and television in Crete. You should also be able to receive the BBC World Service and VOA (Voice of America) without much difficulty on a portable transistor radio, as well as the American Forces' station. Television programmes often include imported English and American series which are subtitled or dubbed into Greek.

Time Difference: Crete is 2 hr ahead of GMT.

Tipping: A service charge is included in hotel and restaurant bills but it is also customary to leave a tip if you are satisfied with the service provided. Taxi drivers and hairdressers expect a 10% tip and waiters about 5%. You should give hotel porters 100 Drs per bag, and your chambermaid 500 Drs when you leave.

Toilets: Public toilets are usually situated in public parks and in town squares – and they can be filthy! Those in bus stations, tavernas and bars may be a bit better but still tend to be of low standards of hygiene. Remember not to flush used toilet paper down the toilet as it will block up the narrow waste pipes characteristic of Greek plumbing. There is always a bin provided for its disposal. It is a wise precaution to carry tissues or toilet paper with you. Avoid the toilets at the monastery at Preveli; the best public conveniences are those on the waterside at Rethymnon.

Tourist Information: The National Tourist Organization of Greece (NTOG), also known as the EOT (Ellinikos Organismos Tourismou), has offices manned by generally helpful, multilingual staff who will provide

information on excursions, accommodation (see **A-Z**), ferry times, etc., as well as useful brochures, maps and timetables.
NTOG offices:
Kriari Street 40, 4th Floor, Chania (0800-1500 Mon.-Fri.); Xanthoudidou Street, Eleftherias Square, Heraklion, tel: 081-222487; on the seafront at Rethymnon, tel: 0831-29148; by the bridge in Agios Nikolaos, tel: 0841-22357; and at the airports (see **A-Z**).
See **Guides**, **Opening Times, What's On**.

Transport: Buses are the cheapest way of getting around the island, although their timetables can sometimes be restrictive and can also change frequently. Hiring a car allows you much more flexibility if you want to explore the island but petrol is expensive. Taxis, especially if you can get together with others to share the cost, are a good alternative both for excursions and for getting from A to B. Hiring a motorcycle or moped can give you greater freedom of movement but be warned – every year there are a large number of accidents due to the poor condition of the roads, lack of experience and carelessness. Quite often it is possible, and fun, to hire local fishing boats to take you to remote beaches and small offshore islands where you can snorkel and sunbathe away from the crowds. See **Airports**, **Buses**, **Ferries**, **Taxis**, **Yachts**.

Traveller's Cheques: See **Money**.

What's On: Free newspapers are published in the main resorts during the summer which are given away at the tourist offices, e.g. *Crete News* in Chania, *This Month Crete* in Rethymnon. These have advertisements for events, restaurants and excursions for tourists. Flyposters are also frequent and will tell you what special entertainments are coming up locally. Otherwise ask at the NTOG office (see **Tourist Information**) or your hotel reception desk. See **Events**, **Newspapers**.

Yachts: Any yacht entering Greek waters is obliged to put into a designated entry point where the yacht's transit log must be handed over to the authorities. In the case of Crete, these are at the provincial capitals which all have marinas. The harbours of Chania, Soudha, Kastelli

Kissamou, Paleochora, Rethymnon, Panormas, Agia Galini, Heraklion, Chersonisos, Agios Nikolaos, Sitia and Ierapetra can all provide fresh water, fuel and electricity. Chania also has a yacht repair service and there is a small repair yard at Agios Nikolaos.

Contact the following for further information:

Chania Marine Club (NOX), Akti Kanari, tel: 0821-24387; Rethymnon Marine Club (NOP), tel: 0831-29881; Agios Nikolaos Marine Club (NAOAN), tel: 0841-22832; Heraklion Café Marina (NOH), Venetian harbour, tel: 081-221128.

It is possible to hire yachts with crews but this is extremely expensive.

Youth Hostels: There are youth hostels in the most popular north coast resorts such as Agios Nikolaos, Chania, etc., but the number changes from year to year so check with the local NTOG office (see **Tourist Information**) to find out if there is one where you want to go. The facilities offered in these are generally very basic and stays are often limited to five days, but conditions are clean, you can often cook your own food and, above all, they are very cheap. Theoretically you will need an International Youth Hostel Association membership card which can be obtained at the Greek headquarters at Dragatsanion Street 4, Athens (if you did not acquire one before you left home). However, the chances are that you will not be asked to produce this.

This book was produced using QuarkXPress™ and Adobe Illustrator 88™ on Apple Macintosh™ computers and output to separated film on a Linotronic™ 300 Imagesetter

Text: Jennifer Bassett
Photography: Phil Springthorpe
Electronic Cartography: Susan Harvey Design

First published 1990 Second Edition 1993

Published by HarperCollins Publishers
Printed in Italy by Amadeus S.p.A.
ISBN 0 00 470037-6

Guidebook information is subject to being outdated by changes to opening hours, prices, and by fluctuating restaurant standards. Every effort has been made to give you an up-to-date text but the publishers cannot accept any liability for errors, omissions or changes in detail or for any consequences arising from the use of information contained herein.
The publishers welcome corrections and suggestions from readers; write to: The Publishing Manager, Travel Guides, HarperCollins Publishers, PO Box, Glasgow G4 0NB.

Samaria Gorge